kevin gerald

by design or default

creating a church culture that works

NELSON BOOKS

A Division of Thomas Nelson Publishers

Since 1798

www.thomasnelson.com

Published in Nashville, Tennessee, by Thomas Nelson, Inc.
www.thomasnelson.com

Nelson Books titles may be purchased in bulk for educational, business, fundraising, or sales promotional use. For information, please email SpecialMarkets@ThomasNelson.com.

By Design or Default?
ISBN: 1–5995–1030–8

Library of Congress Cataloging-in-Publication Data

Gerald, Kevin.
  By design or default? : creating a church culture that works / Kevin Gerald.
     p. cm.
  ISBN 978-1-59951-030-9 (trade paper)
  1. Church renewal. I. Title.
  BV600.3.G47 2007
  253—dc22

                                                      2006034945

Printed in the United States of America
1 2 3 4 5 6 RRD 10 09 08 07 06

Acknowledgments

First, I want to thank the incredible Champions at Champions Centre who share our vision for an evolving and influential culture that keeps Christ's message uncluttered and attractive in today's society.

Second, I want to thank our leadership team and church staff for helping us navigate the journey each day into new territory. For resisting the temptation to settle into the familiar and pressing forward into fresh concepts and creative ideas. We love doing church with you.

Third, I want to thank the pastors around the world who share our conviction that our greatest responsibility is not to a past generation, but to this generation. You have inspired me with your energy and creativity.

by design or default

creating a church culture that works

Every church has a culture . . .
by design or by default.

Contents

Introduction

➤ What Is Church Culture by Design?

The pastor standing in front of me was angry. "All this talk of culture makes me nervous," he said. Needless to say, my message about the need to intentionally design the culture of our churches had struck a nerve in him. He continued, "At our church we preach the same unchanging gospel that was preached in the early church. And if it was good enough for them, it's good enough for me."

His defensive words sounded familiar. As a second-generation pastor, growing up in a denomination that took great pride in its allegiance to the *old paths,* I knew that voice of reason well. I thought, *How can I help this sincere, hardworking, fully committed pastor know that his church already has a culture?* The question was not whether he wanted culture that was unique to his congregation; the question was (as Dr. Phil would say), "How's that working for you?"

I wanted him to understand that every congregation of believers emanates a pattern of behaviors that communicates their beliefs to others. These social forms, rituals, and methods form a culture that is unique to their social group. Even though churches are established on the central beliefs in the Word of God, there are hundreds of thousands of churches because people cluster together who share similar attitudes, values, goals, and practices based on what they believe is important to them in God's Word.

The question I pose to church leaders and laypeople who care about reaching their communities with the good news of Jesus Christ, is whether or not the culture of their churches is helping or hurting their effectiveness.

Consider, for example, the attitudes and atmosphere of your own church:

- Is the culture of your church in harmony with the message of hope you support?
- Is the culture of your church inviting to newcomers and magnetic in nature?
- Does the environment of your church generate an expectancy of good news or doom?
- Do the people in your church seem generous or impoverished?
- Are leaders and members of your church upbeat and positive?
- Are leaders and members of your church full of life or do they appear to be slowly dying?
- Is the atmosphere of your church happy and hopeful?
- Is your church old and rigid or fresh and flexible?

It is possible that you step into an uncomfortable culture every time you go to church. It is also possible that even your most loyal church leaders find the style and rituals of the church service to be incongruous with their everyday relationship with God. Perhaps you want to see a different culture in your church, but you simply don't know how to change the one you have. Then this book is for you.

Church culture is most often created by *default*. It may come into existence through the life patterns and inherited habits of its founders and continue without much thought or consideration of whether or not some changes ought to be made. Typically a church's culture is rooted in dated traditions and methodologies that appear too sacred to question or require too much effort to update with more relevant practices. As a result, most churches crystallize cultures that memorialize the past and focus their energy into preserving the methods of a previous generation, instead of purposefully serving the needs of the current mission.

For example, Jeff and Sue (not their real names) were pastors of a longstanding traditional church in an older neighborhood that was beginning to fill with young couples. The small membership of the church was comprised mostly of senior adults who had been there longer than Pastor Jeff. Their tradition was to begin at 11:00 a.m. and dismiss by 12:45 p.m. Pastor Jeff suggested to the members that the service times begin at 10:15 a.m. in order to dismiss before noon, so that they could facilitate the younger families whose children grew hungry and tired before the late dismissal. But their "voice of reason" argued, "The service time was fine when *my* children were small, it should be good enough for the next generation."

It had been years since the classrooms had been painted; the outwardly beautiful stone building had a musty smell within—almost like the smell of formaldehyde. When Pastor Jeff presented a budget for some paint and building renovations, the plans were turned down. The voting members of this congregation simply were not interested in spending the money on aesthetic improvements. They couldn't see how the building improvements would help create a church culture that attracted young families.

So many evangelistic ideas that Pastor Jeff had were voted down that eventually he resigned from the church and took a job as a construction carpenter. This large church that is capable of holding hundreds of worshippers continues to shelter about seventy people who are wealthy enough to keep the utilities paid for their own use. This is a good example of church culture by *default*. The church existed because it was deeply rooted in traditions that were meant for another time and another place.

Because laypeople influence the church culture as do its leaders, this book is intended to help both pastors and members engage in the never ending process of creating a purposeful church culture, which flows with the synergy of their vision for reaching the world with the gospel of Jesus Christ.

It is possible to design a culture that supports and champions the message you want to communicate to your city.

It is possible to create a culture that doesn't contradict your everyday lifestyle but compliments all that you do.

It is possible to create a life-generating church culture that exists on purpose with a culture by design.

I am confident of this because I have seen the fruit of leading by design at our church in Tacoma, Washington. Since 1993, we have continued to add enthusiastic members, who love worshipping and serving the Lord together, at a rate of five hundred to six hundred per year.

In this book, I will refer to some of the processes and programs in use at our church, the Champions Centre, but please understand that we don't value programs over our culture. Programs should exist *for* culture rather than culture existing *from* programs.

Choosing to design our culture, rather than allowing an inherited culture to define us, makes it necessary to consistently and frequently evaluate, and sometimes overhaul, programs to determine whether or not they support the culture our leadership is consciously striving to create. That honest evaluation can sometimes lead to tossing out an outdated program altogether. Or a program that has enjoyed some moderate success in the past may be gutted simply because it does not fit the culture we are pursuing for our future, even though in another church, another location, or another city that same program might be foundational to their culture. In other words, our programs and practices should be centered on our culture rather than culture centering on the programs.

> ## Seven Practices of Culture by Design

When a church culture supports and champions the message that its leaders want to bring to the community, the culture strengthens the *impact* of the message and a synergism attracts newcomers to the vitality of the church's light.

I recognize seven practices that have helped us to build our church. These practices can assist you and your church leaders in creating a church culture that lines up with your own vision. These seven practices will be covered in this book:

1. *Create a model for culture-creating leadership.* We will look at the methods successful leaders use to create a culture that is inspiring to followers and assists them in carrying out a corporate vision to reach specific goals.

2. *Define the attitudes and design the atmosphere that will attract people to God.* It's a weighty, but true reality that how God's people represent His kingdom can cause others to see God in a negative or positive manner. Packaging does matter. This is an important concept for church leaders to embrace. The right packaging can make the gospel message and your church much more attractive to the very people you are trying to reach.

3. *Define your church "Missions and Values" to form a constant compass that church members can refer to.* Without first defining the mission and values for the organization, any effort to create a church culture will result in confusion and conflict for the members of the volunteer and leadership teams.

4. *Create the culture of a life-giving platform.* The platform ministries (teaching, singing, musicians) are not more important than other ministries, but they are the most visi-

ble, which makes them the greatest influences in the church. Without a doubt, nothing is as important to the growth and health of the church as a life-giving, love-generating platform throughout your church services. Remarkably, not all churches recognize the incredible potential importance of Sunday's services. The result is that they put far too little effort into the most important day of the week, while wasting valuable time and effort on programs, events, and activities.

5. *Create the culture of corporate competence.* All churches have both a spiritual body and a corporate structure. We have made some wrong administration and staff decisions in my time as a pastor. But I have never valued corporate competence any more than I do today. If anything, the journey has made me more aware of the vital connection between corporate competence and the success of a church in its mission.

6. *Create a culture that embraces the contribution of both men and women.* A gender-friendly culture has an abundant appreciation of both men and women in the church and places a high value on the roles they play. In a healthy church, you should be able to look around and see happy men and women thriving side by side in every area.

7. *Create a team church culture.* The first thing Jesus did when He began His earthly ministry was to recruit a team. We honor God when we unite people toward the purpose of serving and working as a team to advance His kingdom.

A lot of great foundational books have been written for church leaders that expound on spiritual truths or character development. This is not one of those books. These seven practices of creating a church culture are more like pillars than a foundation. However, when placed on a solid foundation, they support the work of ministry by helping to create a culture that complements, instead of contradicts, what the church leaders want to do. This book will help you define a church culture that exists on purpose—a *culture by design.*

Know the Facts about Church Culture

The first fact that every church leader must understand is that every church has a culture either by design or by default. One church will be filled with people who are relaxed and friendly, while another church houses people who are uptight and reserved. One church will have a congregation that is eager to participate in social events and small groups, while another church will have to urge its people to connect outside of Sunday morning service. And even after coaxing, some church groups will resist *any* participation outside of a traditional service.

Some churches are filled with people who are generous in spirit, and it shows in everything they do. They are ready to serve, give, welcome others, and sing . . . there is a spirit of generosity in the house. Other churches are not so generous. The variety of cultures that are developed in church groups is endless. One church might mix different age groups well, while in another the youth don't want anything to do with adults or the older people are critical of youth. Both are identifiable cultures.

Several years ago, I read an article in our local paper about a tiny congregation that was merging with another church after being forced to close its doors for financial reasons. During World War II the church had been a thriving congregation in the center of the city of Tacoma, with families from the surrounding housing development at its core.

Just like Jeff and Sue's church that I mentioned at the beginning of this book, this church continued to do well through the 1950s, although the members did not see a need to develop children's or youth programs as so many others were beginning to do. Ignoring the demographics of the baby boom generation, they steadfastly refused to change the way they "did church." After all, kids had been sitting next to parents on hard wooden pews for years, so why should they change?

But slowly, families began to drift away, and as the children grew up, they left the church and did not return when they had kids of their own. Attending church was a distant memory to many of its previous members, and the now-grown adults saw no value in taking their children back into an atmosphere that was outdated and, frankly, did not hold many fond memories.

When the church members finally met for one last service together, one of the remaining original members, a lady in her seventies, was asked why she thought the church had dwindled to the point where they could no longer afford to open its doors. She sadly replied, "Well, I guess after the kids grew up and went away there was even less need to change the way we did things. Why start a children's ministry when there were no kids? And we all just started getting old and dying off. Now we are down to just a few of us old ones, and there just didn't seem to be any point in keeping the doors open anymore."

This church is a prime example of how a culture by default develops. Whether thought out or not, its outdated culture eventually led to the demise of the church. It was a culture that failed to progress, a culture that failed to realize that families wanted something more for their children than they themselves had received in the church. They also failed to recognize that they could no longer count on attendance from the surrounding neighborhoods as the core of their congregation.

Fifty years ago, it was not a normal practice to drive more than a couple of minutes outside of a neighborhood to go to church. The church on the corner served the blocks and community around it. It was just unimaginable that someone would put their family in the car and drive miles and miles just to go to church. But today, large and growing churches frequently draw members from surrounding cities; people are willing to drive many miles and spend a considerable amount of time to be a part of a church that serves their needs.

Churches that counted on keeping their doors open based on past operations have ended up like the one in Tacoma which finally had to sell its building. They failed to develop a culture that kept up with the times and met the needs of today's society.

Someone *will* create the culture of your church. Hopefully the culture will be designed with a specific purpose by its leadership. But in churches where leaders do not define a vision for its culture, the personality of the church will be formed by default, chance, and circumstance. Without a predetermined set of objectives, people will drift into titles and responsibilities that leadership would never consciously appoint as team leaders. In those cases, even church members will wonder how these default leaders became authorities in the church.

When the designated leadership of the church doesn't consciously design and create its culture, they are not leaders at all. Instead, they become managers of a culture that is frequently at odds with their personalities and values. The result is that they will constantly hit walls of opposition and not know why. The rates of burnout, dropout, and flake out of both church pastors and church volunteers are abysmally high, and much of it can be attributed to the lack of culture by design.

Leaders cannot thrive in a culture that is inconsistent with who they are and how they think. The default culture wears on the leader and creates health or moral problems, emotional stress, and eventual resignation. It's not pleasant working in a culture that is not congruent with who you are as a leader; and it can be downright miserable.

➤ Your Culture Is Your Packaging and Presentation of the Gospel

The second notable fact about the culture of a church is that the culture is revealed in the church's packaging and presentation of the gospel. Note the words of the greatest church planter of all time, the apostle Paul:

> Even though I am free of the demands and expectations of everyone, I have voluntarily become a servant to any and all in order to reach a wide range of people: religious, nonreligious, meticulous moralists, loose-living

immoralists, the defeated, the demoralized—whoever. I didn't take on their way of life. I kept my bearings in Christ—but *I entered their world* and tried to experience things from their point of view. I've become just about every sort of servant there is in my attempts to lead those I meet into a God-saved life. I did all this because of the Message. I didn't just want to talk about it; I wanted to be *in* on it! (1 Corinthians 9:19–23 MSG, emphasis added).

My observation is that most of the people whom we assume are rejecting the gospel are not rejecting the gospel at all, but rather they are rejecting the *packaging* of the gospel as it is presented to them. When *The Passion of the Christ* was released in movie theaters, it was a tremendous box office success. It seemed everyone *wanted* to experience the gospel on the big screen. On its opening weekend, *The Passion* sold more tickets than the other top twelve movies combined. This came as a surprise to media pundits and Hollywood's elite.

The assumption was that no one outside of the religious world would be interested in paying to see a movie about Jesus. And certainly no one thought that non-Christians would flock to the theaters in droves. But to the surprise of just about everyone, theaters were packed with audiences that were as diverse as can be. Young, old, rich, poor, black, white, educated, and uneducated went to theaters across America to see a movie that blatantly delivered a message straight from the Bible.

If we listen attentively, society is telling us they are open to the gospel, but sadly they may not be drawn or attracted to our churches because of the packaging and presentation that we offer.

When speaking to church leaders, I have often illustrated this point about packaging by placing Bibles in various kinds of shopping and gift packages. The audience doesn't know what is in each package. It is interesting to see how different people respond to the different wrapping of the packages.

For example, the enthusiasm they express over the possibility of winning the jewelry store package is very different to the response they have to a candy store package. You can hear the women gasp with pleasure over the blue bag with the Tiffany & Co. imprint, while men point to the sporting goods package. The same is true with the clothing store packages, the toy store packages, and the computer store packages—different people respond to each wrapping.

I also include an old brown bag in the choices and a new colorful gift bag. But when I pull a Bible out of each one of the bags, it helps church leaders recognize that the package *creates* an opinion of what is in the bag and its presupposed value before the contents are even revealed.

The message of good news that the Christian church wants the world to hear is the same, but that message comes in different kinds of packages to reach different kinds of people. The package that is appealing to some will be repelling to others. But make no mistake, packaging matters. Many churches are so locked into the past that they mistakenly believe the traditional packaging is more important than the message.

Whatever your church culture is will be what visitors see first; your culture is your *packaging* and *presentation* of the gospel. This reality means that people will judge the substance of your church based on what they observe on their first visit, and usually within the first few minutes.

As much as we agree that it is wrong to judge a book by its cover, the reality is that most people do just that. This is why oranges are picked when they are green and then sprayed with chemicals to transform their green color into a vivid and appetizing orange color. Research shows that people will overwhelmingly choose the bright orange color over the green one every time, even when they are told that the fruit is exactly the same in substance, taste, and texture. Their perception is that the orange package contains the best fruit, while the green package contains an inferior fruit.

In the same way that a green or orange peel causes people to accept or reject a fruit, people also will accept or reject the cultural package of a church. Whether it is old or new, homey or corporate, traditional or contemporary, people will respond to the culture that a church embraces and emanates in its outward appearance.

➤ Culture Determines Who Attends Your Church

The third fact is that the culture of your church determines who comes and who stays at your church. The simple truth is that different cultures attract different people. Some churches attract substantially more women than men. Most church leaders whose congregations have a majority of women assume it is purely coincidental, or they assume wrongly that every other church is the same. But in a fair number of cases, a church's appeal to members is unknowingly slanted toward women, rather than men.

A church that lacks the fingerprint of masculinity throughout its culture will inevitably not be as attractive to men. For example, if all of the greeters are women, and the stage is predominately women, and the children's classrooms are staffed only by women, a guest will consciously, or subconsciously, assess the subtle inference that men don't fit into the life of the church and that men's issues and contributions are not valued as much.

Besides attracting certain genders of people, a church also may attract certain social groups. Terms like *child-friendly, seeker-sensitive,* and *age-relevant* are ones that identify and target the specific needs of certain groups of people. The more aware a church is of its target groups, the more conscious that church will be in creating a culture that attracts those same people.

It is helpful to understand that some people leave a church for the same reason that others come to it. For example, some people are annoyed by churches that spend money on playgrounds for children or advertise programs and events for youth. Still others will see that exact focus as appealing because they are at a stage in life when raising their family is of primary importance, and they want a church that places the same high value on their children as they do.

Some people are attracted to a pastor who is more casual in his presentation and teaching style. Others interpret casual as shallow and boring and eventually look for a more intense or formal style of communicator.

Many churches have music teams that wear choir robes to achieve the polished, traditional, and sophisticated look on the ministry platform, but that style doesn't appeal to everyone. Some people see it as stuffy and outdated and prefer a contemporary ministry team on the platform.

I received a letter from a person who described her first visit to our church and who now attends on a regular basis. Initially, what she called "the *mall* atmosphere" of our church surprised them. Our large atrium lobby is complete with a bookstore, coffee shop, children's indoor playground, and a youth game zone; it was not what they expected to see at a church. Although she said she liked it, her family was caught so off guard that they almost didn't come back. Only after visiting a few more times did she realize how all those attractions supported the family and set the atmosphere for the fun, friendly culture of our church.

When I read her letter, I wondered how many others who visited may have not returned because they were not used to our church culture. The very thing that attracts many also may repel some because the packaging of culture determines who comes and who stays at your church.

Another important part of a church's culture will be its racial diversity, or lack of it, in the congregation. At the Champions Centre, we have paid deliberate attention to making sure that all races feel welcome. We have Spanish, Korean, and Russian interpreters in our Sunday morning services. Rather than offer separate services in other parts of the building or at other times, we create a culture that is welcoming to everyone, recognizing that in order to do that we need to make some accommodations.

Our volunteer teams are a reflection of that diversity as well, with a mix of races and heritages reflected across the board. The racial diversity of our church is such a huge part of our culture that no one pays any attention to it; it is not an issue because we have created a church environment where everyone feels welcomed, appreciated, and celebrated.

➤ Whatever a Culture Is – It Grows

The fourth point I want church leaders to be aware of is that whatever the current culture is in the church, it will grow. If you want the culture to change you must communicate deliberate changes, or else the existing attitudes and habits will simply expand.

Teamwork will not grow in a culture of strife, pettiness, and suspicion no matter how much leaders talk about the importance of teams and working together. Synergy results from people working toward a common cause, but that cause may need to be redefined by leadership for the right culture to grow in a church body. Some leaders assume they can simply teach on something and watch it happen. When leaders feel their words are not changing anything, it is typically because their cultures are contradicting the core value of their missions.

A leader will only succeed at achieving his vision for a church body when he strategically designs the culture to be consistent and supportive of the message he wants to teach. For example, the pastor who wants results can't just talk about how wrong it is to gossip; he must advocate zero tolerance for gossip on his team to initiate change in the atmosphere of the church. He can't preach about excellence and progressive attitudes and have dingy, outdated facilities. He can't teach about friendly attitudes and welcoming guests but provide no programs or systems that demonstrate hospitality. Not everything can happen overnight when change is needed, but people need to see steady progress before the cultural message is going to be received and embraced.

➤ A Created Culture Is Always Evolving

The fifth and final point about culture is that a culture by default is old and fixed, but a created culture is always evolving. As a church, Champions Centre is theologically conservative, but culturally liberal. Many churches have changed their theological positions but have remained fixed in their culture. They have the same music, same traditions, and same service styles they had 100 years ago. These churches are ultra conservative when it comes to making any cultural changes within their churches. As their church styles remain very traditional, they have changed their theological positions on important moral, social and political issues. These churches are culturally conservative, but theologically liberal.

The opposite would be true for churches like ours. Our culture is not sacred to us, but our message is. In fact, we feel an obligation to not allow methods or styles to become a sacred cow or unchangeable. If something is outdated and no longer relevant, we quickly abandon our allegiance to it. We are, however, committed to an evolving culture. That is why we are consistently bringing youth into our leadership team. Youth help provide us with fresh eyes with which to examine our approach to ministry. It is not good enough to stay as we are or where we are. When the life of God is flowing in us, we will consistently have fresh songs, fresh vision and a fresh, new way of doing things. Our methods may change, but the message stays the same.

Jesus told the Pharisees that one of their errors was to elevate traditions to the level of doctrine (Matthew 15:6). They had fallen into that pattern because of their desires to hold onto and enforce their cultural traditions as being sacred. It's not easy to constantly adjust to an evolving culture, but it is essential if a church is to remain relevant to every generation.

Be a Culture-Creating Leader

Coach Mike Krzyzewski, the men's basketball coach at Duke University, is legendary. Krzyzewski's players refer to him as Coach K. Coach K has a reputation among the players for teaching them about leadership and the intangibles that go along with the game. Something is working because Coach K has led his team to win three NCAA National Championships.

Although we know him as a great basketball coach, Coach K describes his role in much broader terms: "I am a leader who happens to coach basketball." He explains that his responsibility to the players and the university goes far beyond the game skills he teaches on the court; when his players get out into the workplace, they're armed with more than a jump shot or a dribble. He says to them, "I want you armed for life. I want you to develop as a player. I want you to develop as a student, and I want you to develop as a human being. My life isn't about playing games."

This eight-time national coach of the year was asked how to motivate the unmotivated by a former coach who was working as a juvenile probation officer. Krzyzewski answered, "In our society, there are three words that are used a lot, and they're great, especially if you mean them when you say, 'I love you.' But there are four words that are definitely not said enough by families interacting with kids or with people interacting on your team or on your business team, and they are, 'I believe in you.'"

Coach Krzyzewski then explained there were times when his team became discouraged and disoriented, when they simply needed somebody to look in their eyes and communicate confidence and trust in them. He said, "I find the most powerful message to tell someone in times like that is 'Son, I believe in you. You're not going to do this journey alone.'" Krzyzewski teaches that two are only better than one when two are working together as one. He leads his team through good communication, trust, collective responsibility, caring and pride.[1]

Krzyzewski's game plan is a great example of a big-picture, culture-creating approach to leadership. A great leadership plan establishes the way the team or organization pursues its goals, the standards they adhere to, and the philosophies that guide them in their mission.

Once clear objectives are established, the result is fundamentally predictable because it's based on a clear set of philosophies and values. Having a deliberate game plan is an essential and common trait of all successful organizations. Successful leaders always create a culture that inspires followers, helps them carry out the vision before them, and enables them to reach specific goals.

Notice how specific the following instructions given by leaders to their teams are, and consider how their words literally created a culture in which their followers could operate.

› Jesus Is a Culture-Creating Leader

Jesus called His twelve disciples to Him and gave them authority to do specific things in His name. Then He told His disciples: "Do not go among the Gentiles or enter any town of the Samaritans. . . . As you go, preach this message: 'The kingdom of heaven is near.' . . . Do not take along any gold or silver or copper in your belts; take no bag for the journey, or extra tunic, or sandals or a staff; . . . As you enter the home, give it your greeting . . . . If anyone will not welcome you or listen to your words, shake the dust off your feet when you leave that home or town" (Matthew 10:5–14).

Jesus started with an encouraging word for His followers, but then He gave His "team" specific instructions on where to go and not go, what to take and not take, how to behave at their destination, and what to do when they moved on to the next place. In other words, He did not leave the details of ministry to whatever whim the team *felt* like following, and whatever path they *felt* like taking. He was exhibiting the four skills of true leadership:

- Gather a team around a common cause.
- Motivate them with encouragement.
- Give them directions to follow.
- Send them out to accomplish the mission.

Jesus defined clearly the culture in which the team was to operate. Consider the fact that Jesus instructed His team to leave without taking money. This guideline surely had a huge impact on the team as they went out. He wanted to prove to them that God would provide for them along the way. He knew that God would move people's hearts to make donations and give offerings. This act of stepping out in faith and total dependence upon God was surely a defining part of their culture for this particular mission trip.

The culture Jesus was creating was one of complete trust in God to provide for their needs. He had already told His disciples that the Father would give them everything they needed (see Matthew 6).

But you can imagine that not everyone on the team that day agreed with the decision to take no money, gold, or jewelry to trade. There may have even been discussion about this, or murmured complaints and discussions on the side. But strong leaders need to make decisions based on the big picture and based on the culture in which they want to see their team operate. The Bible does not say that Jesus gathered them and then took a vote. It does not say that He presented them with three options and probable scenarios. He was the leader, and He was setting the pace for the team.

Without a clear plan, the disciples might have gone into areas where Jesus already knew they would not be received, and they would have missed areas where God had prepared the hearts of the people to receive them.

Without the leadership skills of Jesus, the disciples could have wasted years by staying near homes or towns where their message was not heard in the mistaken hope that eventually everyone they met would welcome them and receive their message of good news.

Without their leader's clear directive, the gospel and the establishing of the church could have ended in a single town.

This example of the specific way Jesus sent out His team illustrates how futile it is for church teams to let their ministries evolve by default, but many church leaders simply lack the understanding of how to initiate culture by design. Culture by design, instead of by happenstance, will always lead to a more productive and successful ministry.

Leaders must give clear directives. Team members need to know what the mission is, what the values are, and how they are supposed to operate. Clear initiatives work for businesses and families too. In the next section, I will share a few more examples of effective leadership skills that can be adapted to better supervision of church teams.

> The Wal-Mart Environment

Sam Walton, founder of the largest retail chain of stores in the world, addressed one hundred thousand Wal-Mart associates via satellite in the mid-1980s, "Now I want you to raise your right hand, and remember what we say at Wal-Mart, that a promise we make is a promise we keep. And I want you to repeat after me, 'From this day forward, I solemnly promise and declare that every time a customer comes within ten feet of me, I will smile, look him in the eye, and greet him, so help me Sam.'"[2]

As you can see from the fruit of his life, Sam Walton knew how to inspire followers with a specific culture-creating model of leadership. He created a structure that supported the culture he was trying to create, and he defined the type of people he wanted to recruit to carry out his vision.

Walton once said that, "Capital isn't scarce; vision is." He established a simple motto of "Giving, Helping, Doing . . ." that his associates could easily follow. Even though Sam Walton died in 1992 and Wal-Mart, as a corporation, has made mistakes, his company continues to be one of the nation's leading corporations in diversity development, charitable contributions, and leadership education, and has been listed for several years on *Fortune* magazine's lists of "Most Admired Companies in America," including one year at number one. The Wal-Mart Corporation still maintains this claim: "We're committed to the communities we serve. We live here, too. And we believe good, works."

At one point in his life, Walton was the world's richest man. His Wal-Mart stores now operate in Mexico, Canada, Argentina, Brazil, South Korea, China, and Puerto Rico. Sam Walton's visions were indeed successful. In his biography, *Made in America: My Story,* Walton outlines what he feels are the ten commandments of business:

1. Commit to your goals.
2. Share your rewards.
3. Energize your colleagues.
4. Communicate all you know.
5. Value your associates.
6. Celebrate your success.
7. Listen to everyone.
8. Deliver more than you promise.
9. Work smarter than others.
10. Blaze your own path.

Walton also said, "Outstanding leaders go out of their way to boost the self-esteem of their personnel. If people believe in themselves, it's amazing what they can accomplish." His words are full of wisdom that can be applied to building teams at any business and church organization.[3]

> ## The Disney Corporation

The Walt Disney Corporation is another example of an organization that has created a purposeful culture by design. Its mission from the beginning was to design a family-friendly entertainment company. It began with cartoons and now encompasses a media empire and theme parks around the world. The purpose of the company has not changed substantially, even as they have added other business ventures that are very different from simply creating cartoons for kids.

Because Walt Disney defined his company's original *mission*, and because his team members remained true to their *purpose*, the corporation has been able to grow, expand, and change with time while maintaining integrity with the stated core values.

In order to keep the gigantic organization on track and in line with the mission and values that define their culture, Disney requires every single employee, no matter what level or position he or she holds, to attend a new employee orientation class (also known as Disney Traditions), taught by the faculty of Disney University.

Disney University is the company's own internal socialization and training organization. Disney designed the course so that new members of the

Disney team can be introduced to the traditions, philosophies, and organizational structure that determine the way they do business. New hires at the Disneyland business experience a multi-layered training program where they quickly learn a new corporate language. Creative ways are used to communicate the culture of Disney to the team. For example:

- Employees are "cast members."
- Customers are "guests."
- A crowd is an "audience."
- A work shift is a "performance."
- A job is a "part."
- A job description is a "script."
- A uniform is a "costume."
- Being on duty is being "onstage."
- Being off duty is "backstage."

This special language reinforces the framework of the Disney culture. The orientation is credited with much of the outstanding success Disney has had in maintaining a culture consistent with the original Disney theme and ideology.[4]

➤ New York City

In the 1990s when Rudy Giuliani took office as the mayor of New York City, the crime rate was at an all-time high. His advisors suggested he implement a strategy called the "broken window" theory.[5] The idea was that the serious crime rate would drop if law enforcement focused *first* on relatively minor problems like graffiti, panhandling, bullying, domestic disputes, etc. The goal was that even a broken window should be repaired within twenty-four hours, thereby sending a message of response, order, and law enforcement to the community.

The average person's perception of local law enforcement was enhanced greatly because the results were visible in their everyday lives. And the criminals noticed, too. The plan worked better than anticipated, and not only did overall crime drop 57 percent, more violent crimes were reduced 65 percent as well.[6] The city that was once infamous for its dangerous streets has been recognized by the FBI as *the* safest large city in America for several years in a row, and by 1999, a Zagat survey revealed that New York City was once again the top tourist destination in the country.[7]

For years, law enforcement had preached its sermon that crime doesn't pay, but it seemed that no one was listening. It wasn't until the results became tangible that the community felt the influence of a culture-creating leader who knew how to change the environment, and thus change the behavior of the people.

As long as petty crime was not dealt with, *all* crime grew. But when broken windows were being repaired right away, the sense of security and neighborhood pride grew. And criminals took notice as well, reasoning that the enhanced law enforcement made the area an undesirable location in which to continue their illicit activities. It was easier for them to move on to a place where no one *seemed* to care what they did.

> ## A Case for Cultural Planning

The culture-creating principles of these time-tested leaders also work in the church. Whatever habits and practices are accepted as normal for your church will become the culture that continues to grow there. Positive people attract more positive people. Negative people attract more negative people because they are not comfortable with positive people. Rarely will a negative person change and become positive; most often he or she will leave that positive atmosphere altogether and go in search of people who support negative attitudes. Pity parties are no fun if no one attends. Leaders who understand the principle will guard the atmosphere in their church, and they will gather, motivate, equip, and send a team of people who have the attitudes and actions that support a positive atmosphere. I always notice in my travels when I leave the extremely healthy and prosperous culture of one city and enter a severely depressed culture in another. Sometimes the cities may be close neighbors. There is a palpable transition when leaving one and entering the other.

All cities have some things in common, and they all have opportunities and challenges. But the *leadership* will determine the financial, moral, and spiritual health of that city. All you have to do is look at a city's culture and you will know whether it has had good leadership or not. Sometimes it is the *lack of leadership* altogether that has defined the culture of a region.

Within the sprawling suburbs of Seattle there are many smaller cities and towns. Only a few miles separate some cities, and often there is only one small sign to indicate when you are leaving one town for another. But there are many major differences in the prosperity of the various areas and towns surrounding Seattle.

For example, thirty miles to the south, the city of Lakewood sits among creeks, lakes, evergreen trees, and the shores of Puget Sound. But it has only been incorporated for less than a decade. Prior to incorporation, the region had one of the highest crime areas in the state. Despite the fact that there were the same number of businesses and homeowners as several neighboring towns, some of the towns were even less attractive. Normally, the crime rate and the number of people weigh heavily in the financial picture and outlook of a city.

And Lakewood had an added advantage from its close proximity to military bases and long-standing, timber-related businesses. The lack of a central city government, however, left the culture of the area to the whims of a county government. What grew was not good: unrestricted and unmonitored low-income housing, homegrown businesses in the midst of residential neighborhoods, sprawling urban signs and billboards, adult entertainment businesses, unkempt public roadways, and a lack of park planning and funding.

On the other hand, several other towns voted to incorporate in the 1950s, '60s and '70s, and those areas grew by purposeful design under the watchful eye of their city governments. Eventually, Lakewood decided to change the culture of the area through a grassroots movement of local homeowners. Although it took several tries, eventually the area voted to incorporate as a city.

The initial changes that the new city government enacted were not welcomed at first. Suspicious homeowners and businesses were used to doing whatever they wanted to do. Taxpayers were worried about added costs for fire and police. However, as order and improvements materialized, residents relaxed and began supporting the change. Neighborhood watch groups reported unprecedented turnouts, as much as 85 percent of the residents of a community, at quarterly meetings with police representatives. High crime areas were cleaned up, parks were developed, and city roads were improved. Streetlights were added, a new city hall was built, and a bankrupt local mall was turned into the Lakewood Towne Centre.

The progress has been slow and steady, but declining crime statistics are proof that good leadership can change the culture of a city. Property values have increased, businesses are making a profit, and new ones continue to move into the city. The modern and well-thought-out town center has become the hub of the city. Three brand new fire stations have been built, and the city now has its own police force instead of "renting" officers from the county sheriff. Lakewood is once again a city that has pride.

Cultural leadership has the same impact on the church. Opportunities and challenges exist for all churches; good leadership will ultimately be reflected in the culture that develops in the church.

➤ *Be* a Culture-Creating Leader

Leadership is not a task or a project; leadership is strength of mind and a prevailing mood of spirit. Most often leadership is thought of as something you do, but my experience is that leadership can be better understood as *being* rather than *doing*.

Be enthusiastic. Be full of God-ideas. Be full of vision. Expect God to solve problems. Soon others will want to *be* like you, and the culture you were hoping to create will take shape. The distinct difference in culture-creating leadership is that it not only teaches but also models and cultivates a life-giving spirit—a spirit of encouragement, a spirit of confidence.

Once you recognize the power of *being,* it's then a matter of developing ongoing, never-ending habits that support a life of leadership. Some things I've done to help me are in my book *Developing Confidence.* There are many habits you can develop that will help you *be* a person who can naturally carry encouragement and confidence in your spirit. Part of *being* a life-giving leader is learning to live healthy and keeping yourself built up. This requires intelligent use of your time, physical exercise, discretion on who you are and hang out with, a sensible diet, laughter and lots of good mental and spiritual food for growing a positive attitude.

History tells us that Abraham Lincoln had a melancholy personality that often caused him to drift into low moods in his younger years. Along the way, some significant changes took place, and he became a much brighter and more optimistic person. He once stated that, "most people are about as happy as they make up their mind to be." What Lincoln realized is that our attitudes change when we change our choice of thoughts. This same president was criticized during the Civil War for gathering his staff in the evenings and telling jokes while the nation was in severe crisis. When criticized, he explained that this was how he kept himself from despair and rejuvenated his soul. His choice to laugh was a source of strength. Laughter as a strength-builder wasn't Lincoln's original idea. It was God's, "a cheerful heart is good medicine . . ." (Proverbs 17:22 NIV).[8]

When God was giving a one-on-one leadership seminar to Joshua, He said, "Be strong and courageous, for you will lead my people to possess all the land I swore to give their ancestors" (Joshua 1:6 NLT). God told Joshua to *be* strong and of good courage. Notice how God was focusing on Joshua's spirit or disposition of mind. It was as if He was implying that the people Joshua was to lead would pick up on his spirit and imitate Joshua's state of mind.

Joshua succeeded in *being* the right man to lead God's people at a time when nations were making war against them. After defeating the five remaining kings who had set their armies against Israel, Joshua created a culture in which Israel could thrive, telling them exactly what God had told him: "Do not be afraid; do not be discouraged. Be strong and courageous. This is what the LORD will do to all the enemies you are going to fight" (Joshua 10:25).

So much of what we hear in leadership development focuses on what leaders *do* instead of who they are. Although our doing is essential to the work that we must get done, the essence of leadership (the part of us that people connect with and respond to) is not in what we do but in who we are. *We are not human doings; we are human beings.*

Joel Osteen, pastor of Lakewood Church in Houston, currently the nation's largest church, is commonly referred to as the "smiling preacher." There is no doubt that a major ingredient of his leadership is that people are drawn to him because of his spirit. If you observe him you will agree that he has a genuine, upbeat, and faith-filled spirit. He smiles a lot and has an optimistic outlook on life.

In and of itself, that is not sufficient to lead thousands of people, but it's what opens the door and gives him the opportunity to present his message. He has done a fantastic job of connecting with the hearts and minds of millions of people through his television ministry. Although much of the world now admires what Joel and his wife, Victoria, are doing, it is safe to say that what he is *doing* has grown out of his *being*. He had that refreshing, happy smile and upbeat spirit long before he had a church that seated 16,000.

Fearlessness and courage is a state of being, not doing. Some good examples of fearless, courageous leaders can be seen in history. Picture William Wallace (you may know him from the movie *Braveheart*) inspiring his countrymen to fight against England's invasion in one of Scotland's darkest hours.

Envision Martin Luther King when he said, "I have a dream that one day this nation will rise up and live out the true meaning of its creed: 'We hold these truths to be self-evident: that all men are created equal,'" thus creating a new culture for America where all social and ethnic groups embrace diversity.

Envision the former prime minister of England, Sir Winston Churchill, intent on finding leaders to rally against Nazi domination, with head high repeating those famous words: "Never give in. Never give in. Never, never, never, never—in nothing, great or small, large or petty—never give in, except to convictions of honor and good sense. Never yield to force. Never yield to the apparently overwhelming might of the enemy." His speech is remembered as "Never Give Up." Those simple words were not eloquent. His *plan* was not what awakened the people's courage—it was the *spirit of his leadership* that people responded to whole-heartedly.

A Crisis Is a Culture-Creating Opportunity

A friend of mine who was in his first year as a head pastor called me to discuss an exodus of people from his church. I heard the disappointment in his voice as he experienced the pain of the first families leaving his small congregation. He shared with me his plan to have a meeting and inform everyone else in the core church about the departing families.

After listening, I asked, "What are you going to do at the meeting?"

He said, "I'm going to tell everyone about the disagreement the people who left had with us as pastors." Basically what he really wanted to say was, "I'm not really a bad guy!"

After a few minutes, I was able to convince him that the real need to stabilize the remaining members was not going to be met by explaining to them that some had chosen to leave the church. The real solution was leadership; it was a great opportunity for him to dig into his spirit as a leader and impart direction, hope, enthusiasm, and vision to the congregation that had made him their pastor. He took my advice and did that; later he called me again to share his excitement about the response of the people.

I'm certainly not insinuating that sharing information is not important when leading people. But I am saying that it is not enough on its own to inspire followers to a cause. People don't want to hear what is wrong; they want to hear what is right!

Perhaps history's best example of this is in the midnight ride of Paul Revere. Most people don't realize that another rider named William Dawes also made a ride that night. Dawes took a different route than Paul Revere but carried the same alerting message that the British were invading the colonies. Revere's delivery that night was remembered, but Dawes' participation was nearly forgotten. The same thing happens in churches everyday; some leaders get a great response to their message while others get no response even though the message is the same.

A primary reason some churches are filling their sanctuaries, while other congregations are dwindling, is in the *spirit* of the leader. Great leaders have a leadership spirit that motivates, compels, and inspires followers. Without the spirit of leadership in a person, plans, messages, hard work, and worthy causes are simply not enough to inspire followers.

If you want people to follow you, you must first define where you want to take them, and then enjoy living in that place yourself. When you do this, people will naturally gravitate toward you and allow you the privilege of being a leader.

3

Create an Attractive Atmosphere

Although there are numerous reasons for strategically creating a healthy church culture, the ultimate goal must be to draw our generation to God. It's a weighty but true reality that we can represent God's kingdom in a way that causes others to see God as less or more attractive. This is an important concept for church leaders to embrace.

The apostle Paul wrote extensively on church culture. He gave specific illustrations of how believers should treat others with love and respect. He explained, "So that in every way they will make the teaching about God our Savior attractive" (Titus 2:10). Again, in Philippians 1:10–11 (MSG), Paul writes, "Live a lover's life, circumspect and exemplary, a life Jesus will be proud of: bountiful in fruits from the soul, making Jesus Christ attractive to all, getting everyone involved in the glory and praise of God." Paul is telling believers that what they do causes others to see Christ as less or more attractive.

We often use the phrase "diamond in the rough" to describe someone whose brilliance and beauty is not yet known. This analogy is drawn from the fact that before the common person can recognize the value of the diamond, a skilled gemologist must free the diamond from the "earthy stuff," the bits and pieces of dirt and rock attached to it, and present it in a way that the average person can comprehend its value. Then and only then can someone who doesn't know much about diamonds recognize its beauty.

There is also "earthy stuff" attached to the gospel message that lessens its attraction for people who don't know the true beauty and value that Christ has for their lives. The peripheral "attachments," which many people have bumped into when they attended church in the past, have disillusioned them and kept them from seeing the overall value of serving God.

Paul's letters to Titus and the believers at Philippi tell us to do everything we can to bring out the beauty of the gospel. We must polish our rough edges to display the brilliance of God's glory in our lives. We must do everything we can to free our message from the things that lessen its attractiveness to a person who has not embraced the church. We must avoid things like outdated traditions, irrelevant messages, weighty and sad atmospheres, church conflict, and strife.

Tom is a good example of someone who needs help in order to see the beauty of God's Word for his life. He was thirty-four years old with children of his own when I first talked with him about getting involved in church again. Since leaving home to go to college, his memories of church as a youth kept him from attending church.

He is not sure how he feels about God, but one thing he is sure of is that he is not excited about going back to the way church was when he was a kid. Even then he felt that the people at church seemed to be stuck in time and were not living in the same world he was facing. He remembered people who always seemed to struggle with life and who were indifferent toward non-Christians. Their negative talk about the world and the carnality of anyone who enjoyed life and modern culture seemed stiff and unloving to him. Even the church building he remembers was cold and bare with no warmth or attractiveness.

The announcements were usually centered on irrelevant events such as trying to get help with a bake sale or needing volunteers to help with the scout program. The pastor's sermons were lecture style and left Tom wondering what he was trying to say and how the message applied to his life and his problems.

Even though Tom now felt a responsibility to introduce his own children to the way of Lord, he sensed that going to church was what he felt *obligated* to do, rather than something he wanted to do and would benefit from. The beauty of the church is something Tom had never really seen. It had been hidden behind an unattractive church culture. Unfortunately, Tom's view of church attendance also became his view of being a Christian—there was simply no attraction.

> **How Attractive Is Your Message?**

One of the most impressive characteristics of Jesus' ministry was that it *attracted* crowds—large crowds—crowds that the Bible calls *multitudes*. They were *drawn* to Him. The Bible says in Luke 2:52

(KJV) that Jesus "increased . . . in favour with God and man." This implies that the more people knew about Him, the more they were *attracted to Him*.

Individuals and churches that recognize the characteristics that made Jesus attractive to the multitudes and incorporate those ingredients into their church culture also will attract people. This contradicts what some Christians assume because they were taught that being Christlike will cause people to *not like* them. This mistaken thought comes from the belief that everyone hated Jesus and this led to His death. In their efforts to be Christlike, they assume that being unattractive to people in the world is a good thing.

The truth is, the only people who didn't like Jesus were a few religious leaders who were threatened by His popularity, but thousands of people followed Him just to hear what He had to say.

Although there are plenty of other things about us all that could make us *unlikable*, an authentic Christlike attitude in our approach to ministry will appeal to people, not repel them. Christlike attitudes will always have an irresistible magnetism on human nature.

Once you see Jesus as a positive, culture-creating leader, then you will recognize His repetitive examples of this in Scripture. He was not antisocial or antigovernment. He never led a revolt or staged a protest. He did teach and practice a way of life that attracted people.

> ## Imagine Your Favorite Place to Dine

Think of your favorite restaurants. We all know that great attitudes and atmosphere in a restaurant will never compensate for bad food, but we also know that bad attitudes and atmosphere can cause great food to lose its appeal. Chances are that your favorite restaurants not only have great food but also a pleasing environment, excellent service, positive attitudes, and clean practices. Considering the needs of a customer is the only thing that will bring and keep business; likewise, people seeking God also are looking for a better life with these same qualities—good food (messages), great attitudes (service), and a pleasing atmosphere (environment).

We have a very large military presence in our region. One day, just after the 2003 war in Iraq had begun, a group of soldiers visited a well-known local restaurant for lunch. Several of my staff members happened to be there as well.

Two older women were already being served in the restaurant when the soldiers were seated at the table next to them. The women immediately called for their server and loudly asked for the soldiers to be moved as the women were very opposed to the war in Iraq, and they did not want to have to look at the soldiers while they ate. The server did not know what to do and instead of taking action on her own, she went to her manager to find out what to do. Several tense minutes went by in the restaurant until the manager finally appeared. He asked the soldiers to move and told them that their presence was offensive to the women. Sitting nearby, however, were my staff members and several other tables of people who all heard the exchange and were appalled at the management's response. They felt that the women should have been asked to move, flatly been refused, or even asked to leave themselves.

Later, my staff heard that one of the other observers called a local talk radio station with the story, and within hours the restaurant was flooded with calls! Business dropped in the ensuing days as the story of how they treated the soldiers spread through the community. Finally, a local listener to the radio station made an offer to pay for the involved soldiers and their commanding officers to eat at the restaurant for free. The soldiers accepted the offer, and the restaurant set aside a special area for the day of the visit. The talk about the incident eventually died down after the soldiers were honored, even though it was a result of a radio listener who was not involved in the original incident.

The restaurant could have stemmed the damage by reacting during the initial confrontation, but they chose to do nothing. In other words, they were allowing a cultural concept of their business policy to evolve *by default,* and it was one that said soldiers were not welcome there. This was probably not true, but their inaction and failure to address a one-time incident was quickly beginning to define their culture and possibly affecting their future business as well. They did too little, too late. Even after the special dinner, there remained a lingering doubt about the restaurant's commitment to the military community, and one can only speculate how that negative publicity may have harmed their business. That reputation was not one they set out to create. Inaction created a reputation by default, not design.

The apostle James was a culture-creating leader who also wrote extensively about how we believers should treat people who come into our meetings. In chapter two, James says that we should never show favoritism. He wrote, "Suppose a man comes into your meeting wearing a gold ring and fine clothes, and a poor man in shabby clothes also comes in. If you show special attention to the man wearing fine clothes and say, 'Here's a good seat for you,' but say to the poor man, 'You stand there' or 'Sit on the floor by my feet,' have you not discriminated among yourselves and become judges with evil thoughts?" (James 2:2–4).

James went on to explain that God has chosen those who are poor in the eyes of the world to be rich in faith and to inherit the kingdom He promised those who love Him, so we should never insult the poor. He pointed out that it is the rich who exploit people and drag them into court.

"If you really keep the royal law found in Scripture," James continued, "'Love your neighbor as yourself,' you are doing right. But if you show favoritism, you sin and are convicted by the law as lawbreakers. For whoever keeps the whole law and yet stumbles at just one point is guilty of breaking all of it" (James 2:8–10).

If we are acting in humility, we will treat everyone with respect and value, regardless of whether or not their appearance tempts us to believe otherwise. Jesus demonstrated the ultimate act of humility by laying down His divine rights to become a servant of God's grace. The apostle Paul's view of humility is paraphrased in the following passage:

> Don't push your way to the front; don't sweet talk your way to the top. Put yourself aside, and help others get ahead. Don't be obsessed with getting your own advantage. Forget yourselves long enough to lend a helping hand.
> Think of yourselves the way Christ Jesus thought of himself. He had equal status with

God but didn't think so much of himself that he had to cling to the advantages of that status no matter what. Not at all. When the time came, he set aside the privileges of deity and took on the status of a slave, became human! Having become human, he stayed human. It was an incredibly humbling process. He didn't claim special privileges. Instead, he lived a selfless, obedient life and then died a selfless, obedient death—and the worst kind of death at that: a crucifixion (Philippians 2:3–8 MSG).

Imagine how full our churches would be if we all treated each other as Jesus treated us!

> ## Attractive Attitudes
> ## and Atmospheres

I mentioned in chapter one that a few years ago I started pondering the question: "Is it possible that many people are not rejecting the gospel but are instead rejecting the packaging and presentation of the gospel?" And if the answer is yes, what can we do so that our message is not unattractive but attractive—not repelling but magnetic?

The truth is that a person can have the most fantastic testimony of what God has done for him or her, but no one will be interested in hearing the story if his or her attitude and lifestyle is not attractive as well. The apostle Peter wrote: "It is God's will that your good lives should silence those who foolishly condemn the Gospel without knowing what it can do for them, having never experienced power" 1 Peter 2:15 (TLB).

A church can have brilliant musicians and well-educated preachers, yet still not have a "magnetic field" in its atmosphere that draws people into worship. Presenting the gospel with the wrong attitude is like serving an incredible steak dinner on the lid of a trashcan.

We cannot save anyone ourselves, but we can create an atmosphere filled with Christlike attitudes that makes the gospel attractive to the world. We can, and should, make it hard for someone to choose to go to hell.

The Scriptures at the beginning of this chapter show us that there is a way to make the teachings of God attractive and a way to make Jesus Christ attractive. Based on that thought and some observations of the way Jesus attracted crowds, let's look at attitudes that create positive atmospheres that attract people to God.

➤ Serving with Humility

The first atmosphere that makes a church culture attractive is when its leaders demonstrate an attitude of humility. The word humility translated in the English language lacks the full meaning of the biblical text. But based on its root word *humble,* humility is best defined by what it is not: it is not proud or haughty, not arrogant or assertive. A humble person defers to the needs of another, not out of oppression or inferiority, but out of assertive love. A person with humility shows respect and esteem to all others, both prestigious and obscure, with an ingratiating regard for another's wishes.

Some people's idea of humility is that it is the same as having low self-esteem, or a low opinion of oneself. This is not true. People with false humility operate out of the belief that to lose at life is to somehow please God. And the corresponding idea to this concept of impoverishment is that to strive for success in life is to sin; therefore, being poor and having a life full of financial problems and low self-esteem is something to be desired. The trouble with this logic is that self-degradation and deprivation is not a lifestyle that is attractive to very many people. If poverty and passiveness is the model for spirituality, the average person will question why anyone would want to embrace Christianity.

For many years, mainstream media latched onto this substandard image of Christianity, and popular television shows and movies portrayed this erroneous concept as the norm among true believers and the church world in general. The only broadcast images of Christianity that differed from this worldview were those of ministries and televangelists, many of whom operated out of greed and wrong motivation. Countering either image is difficult, but it must be done in order to offer the nonbeliever a legitimate and attractive view of Christianity.

Thankfully, there are many Christians now working in Hollywood and in media broadcasting who are influencing screenplay writers and producers to give a more accurate view of those with faith. But lost people need to see their neighbors and coworkers demonstrate Christlike concern toward them. They need to be able to attend local churches where Christlike attitudes fill the atmosphere.

In the pure biblical meaning, people with humility don't think less of themselves—they just think of themselves less. The humble person's outlook in life does not ask, "What can you do for me?" rather, "What can I do for you?" People and churches with attitudes and atmospheres where this kind of true humility can be seen and felt will inevitably attract people to them.

Jesus looked for opportunities to make people's lives better, and they could *feel* that purpose from Him. When in His presence, and when listening to Him teach, they sensed that He was encouraging them to strive for a better and more enriching life. In fact, He said, "I have come that they may have life, and have it to the full" (John 10:10).

Humility is not having an inferiority complex or low self-worth; in fact, a person must have a positive self-view before he or she can walk in true humility. A person with sincere humility understands that he or she has much to offer others, yet he demonstrates love and enriches other people to make their lives better. A truly humble believer sees his or her own worth in the eyes of the Lord, but also recognizes the worth of others as valuable in the eyes of God. Humility is an attitude that demonstrates love, serves and gives to enrich other people, and helps to make other peoples' lives better.

But this positive self-view requires a delicate balance in order to avoid the temptation to become overly self-centered, instead of Christ-centered. I've been to some churches where everyone, including the people on the platform, appear to be far too conscious of their own image. (We will talk more about this in chapter four.) When the singers sing, it is obvious that singing is all about *their* performance; and when the preacher preaches, it is all about *his* delivery.

One can sense when it is all over that the only thing the ministers wonder is how did *they* do? Did we like *their* singing? Were we impressed with *their* message? I'm not saying they are bad people, or even that they are intentionally self-serving, but the image that they portray certainly *seems* to be self-serving and self-motivated.

True humility is something to be desired, and any church that succeeds in cultivating humility will focus on enriching people's lives. They will have an irresistible appeal to those who attend.

The attitude of humility, when it is present, fills an unexplainable need in the heart of humanity. There is something in human nature that causes people to be attracted to other people who have a genuine concern for them. A church group that has a visible concern for people will grow. That spirit of humility manifests in many ways, but one thing is sure—it is always attractive.

➤ Endorse God's Plan of Abundant Life

The second positive attitude the leaders should try to create in their churches is an atmosphere that *endorses life*.

Jesus always gave life "a big thumbs up!" He knew life had troubles, but He stayed off the "ain't-life-awful" bandwagon. In fact, He encouraged people who were in imperfect situations to "be of good cheer." He told a paralytic to be of good cheer while the man was still ill (Matthew 9:2 KJV). He challenged His disciples to be of good cheer while they were in a raging storm at sea (Matthew 14:27 KJV). In one of His most famous messages, Jesus told His listeners that they will *always* have trouble in this world but to "be of good cheer" because He has overcome the world (John 16:33 KJV).

Jesus endorsed life as a God-given gift, worthy of cheerfulness and optimism. But many of the gospel songs in previous generations have expressed an indifference toward life on earth. Perhaps the struggles that were more common to their generation caused believers to sing lyrics like, "Goodbye World, Goodbye" or "Lately, I've got Leavin' on My Mind." That theme is very different than the theme in "Celebrate" or "Jesus Came to Give Us Abundant Life."

The insinuation of the previous songs was that "this ole world is a rotten place, and we can't wait to get out of here," while the latter theme emphasizes God's passion and love for the world and all of us who live in it. One set of songs sends a message that life is too hard to take much more of it, and the other sends a message that endorses life and celebrates what God has given us, right now.

When man is indifferent toward life, he is indifferent toward the plan of God that placed him here. Without even realizing it, that indifference will destroy the harmony God intended people to experience as partakers of the life He has given them. Out of that indifference emerges a discontent that causes people to look for an escape through wild partying, excessive drinking, or drug use. Passivity and the risk-taking nature of the drug-induced culture is an attitude that results from feeling as though one has no value, no mission, or no purpose here on earth.

Once life is referenced as having more problems than pleasure, something to be endured rather than enjoyed, the discontented soul begins to spiral downward. The real cure for life's woes can only be found in an attitude and atmosphere that endorses life in the same way that Jesus did.

When people, whose lives have been spiraling downward, come in contact with this attitude and atmosphere of celebration, they experience an invisible pull upward. That upward tug compels them to join the irresistible celebration, and keep that newly found, higher outlook on life.

> Exude a High Value on Individuals

The third attitude and atmosphere that causes people to return to church is when people are reassured of their value.

Negative media messages, cultural agendas, work and family-life situations often plunder people of their confidence and sense of self-worth every day. This constant onslaught of messages and innuendos undermine people's feelings of personal value. When consistently exposed to the perfection of ready-for-camera makeup, filters, and transplants, many people subconsciously view themselves as less than acceptable. They may not even realize where their lack of self-worth originated.

Jesus, however, affirmed people consistently and spoke to them in a positive manner. We will talk more about this reality in chapters four and six, but it's worth mentioning here to emphasize the magnetic force of affirmation. A primary example of God's desire to affirm us is when Jesus taught the parables of the lost coin, the lost sheep, and the lost son to emphasize that every person is important to God (see Luke 15). A paraphrase of Jesus' lessons would be, "If a woman loses a coin, she doesn't rest until she finds it . . . if a shepherd loses a sheep he goes out into the night looking for it. If a father is away from a son, he rejoices when the son returns. In the same way your heavenly father places high value on you."

At the risk of using a cliché, "we gotta raise the bar" if we are going to represent God's love and viewpoint of humanity. People need to hear and receive a message that builds their self-confidence, encourages them to be all that God wants them to be, and supports them when they strive for more in life.

Our church culture supports an atmosphere where developing one's gifts and leadership ability is encouraged. At the Champions Centre, we have a leadership school called Wisdom for Life that embraces this philosophy. The daytime program is an intensive two-year, leadership training program where students are able to learn about ministry and are challenged to develop leadership skills. This is all done in a positive environment where they learn through Scripture about their value and worth. The principles taught are applicable to leaders in the marketplace or in society, as well as in the church. The fast track program at night teaches these same principles, although the students are primarily a little bit older and most work full time during the day.

Nancy is a typical student in the fast track program. Ten years ago, she was living with her boyfriend and her two young children in a low-income housing project. Her only goal at that time was to survive until the next party—or the next catastrophe, whichever came first.

She was introduced to the gospel and to the Champions Centre through an outreach program we offer to children in the community. Her two sons participated in the program every week. Nancy began to see changes in her sons and was attracted to the positive message that her boys were hearing. Eventually, she began attending the church, and her confidence and self-esteem rose dramatically.

Conviction also came. Shortly after attending our services, Nancy and her boyfriend were married by one of our staff pastors. As she continued to grow in her knowledge of God, so did her belief that she was capable of doing great things for the kingdom of heaven.

Nancy decided to enroll in Wisdom for Life and recently received her diploma after two years of night school. She is now one of our full-time staff members; she and her husband bought their first home; her boys are involved in youth leadership; other family members have been saved as well. The change that occurred in Nancy is a result of a positive, life-changing message that she mattered to God, and that He had a great plan for her life. This truth is often heard in the environment at the Champions Centre where we encourage people to enjoy being their best.

➤ Set an Example of Excellence

The fourth attitude that creates an enthusiastic atmosphere is one where excellence is applauded. The idea of excellence is to exceed the normal effort, to go the extra mile, and to offer more than has been requested or expected. The word *excellent* is used in Scripture to describe the nature, power, wisdom, and greatness of God. Paul encouraged believers to focus on what is excellent, saying, "Finally, brothers, whatever is true, whatever is noble, whatever is right, whatever is pure, whatever is lovely, whatever is admirable—if anything is excellent or praiseworthy—think about such things" (Philippians 4:8).

Unfortunately, many churches are the most tolerant places in town for mediocrity. The baptistery water is cold. The paint is worn. The musical instruments are old. The bathrooms are repulsive. Clutter is in the hallways. The children's classrooms are in a musty basement. The amazing thing is that the church leaders can't understand why more people are not coming to their church. So they pray harder, preach harder, and beg harder for their members to bring people to church with them.

These church leaders fail to realize that the facility is the first impression people have of the church and its message! The visitor either consciously or unconsciously judges the church and its ministry by his or her first impression of its atmosphere. In this case, the need is not more prayer; the need is a commitment to an atmosphere of excellence.

Don't let your facilities misrepresent who you are and undermine the excellence of the gospel you preach. A first impression can never be changed. And many times, a second chance is never an option.

One church leadership team in the Midwest devised a plan to evaluate their church building and the impression it gave by connecting with another church in their area. The two pastors agreed to send a team of staff members to each other's churches, but without letting anyone on their own team know about it. They went in hand with a secret list of areas that the pastors wanted to have evaluated.

These details included the entry areas and even the impressions they received when driving into the parking lot. Was it easy to find parking? Did anyone greet them? How hard was it to find the right doors to enter? The secret evaluations continued as they assessed the bulletins, the children's and youth areas, the bathrooms, the adult classrooms, and the sanctuary. As painful as it was to submit to such scrutiny, they came away from the experience amazed at how many things they had simply not considered and at how different an impression they were actually making than the one they *thought* they were making.

However, rather than organizing a step-by-step, department-by-department to-do list, a better solution is to create and communicate an attitude of excellence to everyone who participates. When excellence is a core value, and when your team understands how important it is to maintain high standards, they will consciously evaluate areas they are involved in to see that excellence is always represented.

Instead of establishing rules about what is allowed and what is not, or how to do something and how not to do something, it is better to inspire a culture where excellence is the prevailing attitude. Where people have a disposition of enthusiasm and creativity, they give life to any project. As more people catch this spirit of approach, there is an outward manifestation of excellence that can be seen throughout the facility without anyone having to micromanage it.

The more the spirit of excellence is taught, the more it is caught. An atmosphere of excellence is inspiring to those who attend and helps them to strive for the best in their own homes and lives.

Proclaim that God Is Faithful

The fifth attitude that creates an attractive atmosphere is one that increases people's confidence in God. Many people see God as a God who always says "No." They only know Him as a "Thou-shalt-not" God or a grouchy "No-you-can't-have-fun-happiness-or-blessings" kind of God.

One of the most attractive characteristics of God is His propensity to say "Yes." Paul was among the first to initiate this positive atmosphere of expecting good things from God. He wrote, "But as surely as God is faithful, our message to you is not 'Yes' and 'No.' For the Son of God, Jesus Christ, who was preached among you by me and Silas and Timothy, was not 'Yes' and 'No,' but in him it has always been 'Yes.' For no matter how many promises God has made, they are 'Yes' in Christ. And so through him the 'Amen' is spoken by us to the glory of God" (2 Corinthians 1:18–20).

There is a powerful and compelling appeal in the recognition of God as a Father who loves to do good for His children. There's an amazing attraction in the recognition that He doesn't waver in His thoughts toward us; that He knew us before we were born; and nothing we have done, or have not done, has changed His thoughts toward us. When He looks at us He still says, "Yes! It is good!"

Jesus taught frequently on the "yes" nature of God. For example, when Peter acted surprised that the fig tree Jesus had cursed was withered, Jesus told him, "Have faith in God. Truly, I say to you, whoever says to this mountain, 'Be taken up and thrown into the sea,' and does not doubt in his heart, but believes what he says will come to pass, it will be done for him," (Mark 11:21–23 ESV).

Knowing the hesitation that people felt when it came to following Him, Jesus said, "Don't worry about everyday life—whether you have enough food, drink, and clothes. Doesn't life consist of more than food and clothing? Look at the birds . . . Your heavenly Father already knows all your needs, and he will give you all you need from day to day if you live for him and make the Kingdom of God your primary concern" (Matthew 6:25–26, 32–33 NLT).

When Jesus wanted people to understand the heart of their Father in heaven, He said,

> Ask and it will be given to you; seek and you will find; knock and the door will be opened to you. For everyone who asks receives; he who seeks finds; and to him who knocks, the door will be opened. Which of you, if his son asks for bread, will give him a stone? Or if he asks for a fish, will give him a snake? If you, then, though you are evil, know how to give good gifts to your children, how much more will your Father in heaven give good gifts to those who ask him! (Matthew 7:7–11).

When Jesus' disciples asked Him to teach them how to pray, Jesus gave them the Lord's Prayer as an example. Then He told the parable of the man who responded to his persistent friend who boldly asked for help in the middle of the night. Jesus said that when we pray we should ask and keep on asking, seeking, and knocking until God answers (see Luke

11:9). The parable implies that when God sees our boldness and confidence in His goodness and His ability to provide, He will answer us with a "yes."

Then Jesus confirmed again,

> For everyone who asks receives; he who seeks finds; and to him who knocks, the door will be opened. Which of you fathers, if your son asks for a fish, will give him a snake instead? Or if he asks for an egg, will give him a scorpion? If you then, though you are evil, know how to give good gifts to your children, how much more will your Father in heaven give the Holy Spirit to those who ask him! (Luke 11:10–13).

Imagine that you are able to travel back in time to hear Jesus in person. On a scale of one to ten, if your confidence in God was a two, by the time you got out of a service led by Jesus and His team your faith level would raise dramatically. That's the goal of a church whose mission is to attract people.

A church that communicates confidence in God's ability to meet the needs of His people will see those in attendance gain confidence in God every time they come to a church service. The result is that they will want to come back to the church that builds their faith in God, and they will want to share the inspiration they receive by bringing others to church as well.

➤ Communicate the Life-Giving Nature of God

An attractive congregation is one with a pastor who conveys an attitude and atmosphere that God

51

is a life-giving Father who has more planned for us than we can imagine or think.

How Full Is Your Bucket?—Positive Strategies for Work and Life by Tom Rath and Don Clifton has become a favorite of our church staff. The premise of the book is that we all have an invisible bucket and an invisible dipper, and people either add to our bucket with their dipper or take out of our bucket. As I read the book, I realized that these *exchanges* occur on a daily basis and we either consciously or unconsciously gravitate to people and places that add to our bucket.

Jesus was a *bucket-filler*. That explains another reason people were attracted to Him: He knew clearly that He was a life-giver, not a life-taker, and He boldly proclaimed that as His mission. No wonder people would leave one of His "church services" and enthusiastically tell their friends about it! They were overflowing with the life-giving spirit that came from Him and filled their hearts and souls.

We reviewed five attitudes that a culture-creating leadership can induce: to humbly serve one another, to endorse God's intention to give us an abundant life, to make people feel valuable for who they are, to set examples of excellence in all you do, and to proclaim the good news that God is faithful, trustworthy, and graceful. I want to encourage you to make the extra effort to always have these five attitudes working in you and in the atmosphere of your church so there is a magnetic force at work—a compelling force that reveals the awesome attractiveness of God.

4

Define a Clear Mission and Core Values

Imagine how chaotic and confused society would be if it weren't for our consensus on a fixed landmark called "true north." It's amazing how a simple landmark liberates people of all nations to function efficiently and cooperatively. Whether we are hiking in the mountains with a simple compass or riding in an airplane with a sophisticated navigation system, the awareness of true north is an ongoing point of reference that liberates us to move accurately toward our destinations. Any traveler who loses that point of reference will find himself either paralyzed by confusion or driven to chaos.

Culture by design establishes a compass, by which members of the church can navigate themselves to agreed goals. A design for a culture with purpose must find its roots in the mission and values (MVs) of the organization. Any effort to create a church culture without first defining its MVs will result in confusion and conflict for its members, volunteers, and leadership. But once defined, the MVs are a constant compass to guide and focus the team.

Staff leaders and team members who are equipped with a clearly written mission statement and list of core values are equipped to advance a purposeful culture by design throughout the organization. And clearly defined MVs will help eliminate hurt feelings, confusion, and missed opportunities by a well-meaning, well-intentioned staff that launches programs to Mars when the senior pastor wanted them to go to Saturn.

The MVs of Champions Centre illustrate how we communicate our mission and values to our staff, leadership, new members, and volunteers. We even have these guidelines posted on our website where potential members can evaluate whether or not our goals are in line with their own. Our Mission Statement clearly publicizes our goal: "Equipping People to Live Successful Christian Lives." We also post our Statement of Faith so that members and visitors can quickly explain and discern what we believe.

We even define the methods that we will use to reach our community. As I will share later in this chapter, there are many programs and good works that can be done, but too many efforts can dilute the strength of what your church is uniquely qualified to achieve. It is best to define areas in which you are willing to invest, so that unfruitful programs don't suddenly emerge that drain your budget and focus.

At our church, we limit the focus of our methods of ministry to services at the Champions Centre: corporate events, such as our theatrical productions of the *Great Passion Play* and *Scrooge the Musical*; strategic networks that connect members through small groups; and a team church that offers everyone a place to serve when they are ready to get involved.

Besides writing down our core values, which I will discuss later, it is also important to put into words what we want our church culture to look like. This is known as A Vision Statement.

The Church We See . . .

- Is exciting, growing, and full of life.

- Is equipping people to live successful Christian lives.

- Is a place where people from all walks of life have an inspiring love and commitment to each other.

- Is so relevant and clear that lives are forever changed and people are transformed into champions.

- Is an attractive, confident, and committed place of excellence in both attitude and effort.

- Is a life-giving church.

- Is a TEAM church.

Putting your MVs in a graphic and visual format helps people connect with them in a tangible way.

➤ What Is Your Mission?

A mission statement is the central piece of any successful organization. Everything else centers on the mission statement. It should be succinct, clear, and easy to understand and memorize; in fact, everyone in the organization should be able to recite it without hesitation.

Our mission describes the purpose for which we exist, and one that we rally around. Everyone on our church team wants to equip people to live successful Christian lives.

The mission statement of a church should be more than a nice sounding cliché. It should be a thunderous shout of the pastor's heart. In fact, the only way a congregation will fully embrace a mission statement is when they sense it is also a driving passion of the leader's heart.

As a pastor's son, I grew up in a church-life environment, always hanging out with church people. It didn't take long for me to realize that many in the "saved-from-their-sins" crowd were, more often than not, failing miserably at life. As far back as I can remember, it bothered me that the people at church seemed to be the least successful people in the community. They seemed to constantly struggle with relationship, finance, family, and health issues even more than those who did not attend church. I soon realized that if we, as God's people, were going to influence society, we needed to recognize God's plan for life beyond salvation.

Looking back on it now, I realize that the very thing that bothered me most became my life mission. I have a deep and compelling passion to see people saved and equipped with the wisdom to live successful Christian lives.

➤ Limit Your Methods

Defining your mission also clarifies what your mission is not; and knowing when to say "no" will save you from trying to do too much. One of my greatest challenges in the early years of serving as a pastor was the temptation to try to do everything. We seldom said no to any worthwhile endeavor or ministry. As a result, we started a lot of ministries just because we recognized a need and wanted to help. There was just one problem—as great as they were, these other ministries were not our primary purpose, and eventually we realized they were taking away from our central goals.

Instead of doing a few things really well, we were trying to do everything; and the result was that being so spread out inhibited our energy and our ability to do anything well. I realized that if I wanted to be effective in my mission, I had to keep the main thing the main thing.

Just because we recognize a need, or admire what another church is doing, doesn't mean we are supposed to do it. A good example of this occurred when we set up counseling offices and hired counselors. It didn't take long for us to realize that the demand of time and energy going into the counseling ministry was overtaking our organization's original and primary purpose. Our mission is not to be a counseling center. I just had a heart to help people and had allowed that desire to take our organization down that path. Could we do both? Probably, but not without our primary mission being compromised in some fashion.

Moses had a similar experience when he was counseling people from sunrise to sunset and his father-in-law Jethro said, "What you are doing is not good" (Exodus 18:17). Moses had good intentions, but he simply could not lead the people of Israel to deliverance and be their personal judge at the same time. His primary mission to be a leader of an entire nation was suffering because of his involvement in settling individual disputes.

A similar conflict occurred when we decided to establish a food bank. Our food bank, at one time, served more families in our county than any other food bank. But again we realized that our primary mission was being compromised because of the energy and space required to operate the food bank.

And the food bank was not really serving or supporting our mission of equipping the people in our congregation to live successful Christian lives. We were handing out groceries, but we were not teaching or helping anyone with any practical knowledge on how to improve their lives so that they could go out and get their own groceries.

Now, having a food bank is not a bad thing. We recognize that there are poor people in our community who need help. But instead of trying to duplicate what many other foundations were also doing, we choose to help through donation to these other groups and organizations whose mission is offering food to the needy.

Now we are able to use all of our energy, time, and space in programs and ministries that support *our* mission while retaining the compassionate nature for those less fortunate who need a food bank. I also have found that organizations whose primary mission is to provide food, medicine, counseling, etc., do a better job than our organization because it is *their mission* and *their purpose*.

These worthwhile endeavors, such as counseling and food banks, are examples of how *good* is often an enemy of *great*.

Churches that try to do too much are often good churches that will unfortunately never experience their full potential as a great church because they have not defined their missions and values. Instead of doing a few things with excellence, they do many things with mediocrity.

The desire to do as many good things as possible hinders churches from putting in the extra effort required to be excellent at what they are called to do. They are good in many, many ways, but great in none.

Offering too many services and spreading volunteers too thin happens in some churches because they have a bad case of CADD—Church Attention Deficit Disorder. Leaders with CADD enjoy the rush and excitement of starting a new ministry, but before that ministry matures into a place of strength and excellence they become distracted by the opportunity to start another new ministry. When church leaders are driven by this constant need for the next new outreach, few, if any, of their ministry teams actually excel at what they do. Rather than thrive, they barely survive.

Great churches define their mission and stick to it, and they say no to many worthwhile missions in order to stay focused on the main thing they have been called to achieve. Focused churches excel in creativity to do their mission well, which enables them to stay fresh while doing the same tasks with ongoing excellence. These churches, which are focused on their mission, become high-impact churches serving their communities well.

➤ Define Your Values

Shared values provide people with a common language. Tremendous energy is generated when values are in sync. Enthusiasm and drive are intensified. It is important for leaders to communicate the ideas and principles they stand for, but their values also must be consistent with the aspirations of people. If not, people will not be attracted to the cause.

On the other hand, when people identify with a leader's ideas and principles, they will rally around the cause. The most effective church leaders don't advocate or promote values that are irrelevant to people. Some churches have spiritual sounding values that read like the King James Version of the Bible. They do this in the mistaken belief that the more spiritual or religious they sound, the more inspiring their values will be to people. But if people are confused or have a hard time identifying the value, they will not be inspired by it!

Instead church leaders should aim to:

- Make values something that draws on the best in people.
- Make values consistent with the highest of ideas and dreams.
- Make values easily and clearly communicated.
- Make values consistent with the pastor's highest ideas and principles.

➤ Be Careful Where Your Heart Is

The Word teaches us that our heart will pursue whatever we treasure: "For where your treasure is, there your heart will be also" (Matthew 6:21). In designing a church culture, we found that stating what we value gives team members an opportunity to put their hearts into the tasks that uphold those treasures. The following chart illustrates the seven organizational values that identify our church. I list them to inspire ideas for your own list. At our church, we value:

- Commitment—We value our church members who demonstrate commitment in regular attendance, generous giving, and consistent dedicated involvement.
- Excellence—We value excellence in life and ministry as the only attitude that honors God.
- Leadership—We value the equipping of people to lead, succeed, and increase their influence within our church and community.
- Life—We value a vibrant, positive, exciting church atmosphere that exudes a life-giving spirit through passionate praise.
- Relevance—We value ministry that is current, helpful in life, socially significant, and age relevant, focusing on the interests and needs of people.
- Team—We value teamwork that promotes a shared purpose and is expressed by people of diverse social, economic, and cultural strata connected as the family of God.
- Wisdom—We value the pursuit of wisdom through the Word of God that directs us to a principle-focused, balanced, and successful life.

by design or default?

Our entire leadership team embraces these seven values, and they are evident within the culture of our church. Because we value committed members, our membership continues to grow with people who love supporting the vision we share. Because we treasure excellence, creativity flows through our team members who have a habit of going the extra mile in whatever they do. Because we treasure a positive atmosphere, our hearts pursue a constant faith in God regardless of outward circumstances. And because we value being relevant and full of wisdom, we take time to listen to people and seek God on their behalf.

When a culture is created from the values of a leader's heart, it will be a culture that a leader can be passionate about. A culture based on tangible values is one that others can enjoy assisting the pastor in maintaining. The values become the platform from which leadership teams speak with a clear, consistent sound.

Leadership teams and church congregations are the most harmonious and happiest teams to be a part of when they are brought together by a shared set of values. The clear and consistent communication of values helps to eliminate or minimize the existence of subcultures in the church by getting people on the same page.

Subcultures that are inconsistent with the values of the leader will always weaken the effectiveness of the organization. These subcultures don't typically originate in rebellion; rather they originate by default in organizations that lack design.

This occurred in my own ministry when, without my knowledge or consent, one of our staff pastors began an in-depth ongoing Bible study that immersed itself in answering questions that normal people don't even ask. Teaching independent sessions was not part of his job. He began attracting a small group of people, and eventually they became a subculture completely unlike the rest of our church. They became puffed up, imagining themselves to have superior knowledge, and excluded themselves from the main flow and vision of our mission.

After trying to be accommodating and patient, I finally realized how the subculture this pastor had created was weakening the culture of our church body. I released him, put a stop to the group, and haven't made the mistake of leaving core values undefined since.

You can't always stop people from coming along with an agenda that contradicts the church culture you are trying to establish, but you don't have to make their mission and values a part of your church event calendar—you can at least keep it out of your facility. And certainly you should not pay a staff member who wants to lead or participate in anything that is not congruent with the culture of the corporate vision.

➤ Wisdom Principles for Writing Core Values

Normally the pastor initiates the list of core values for a church culture, but sometimes a leadership team might be called to help define these terms. If you are a pastor or a member of the MV team, you must avoid creating impressive sounding values that do not reflect what the Lord has put in your heart to celebrate.

A core value is not what you *wish* was important to you—a core value is what *is* important to you. If you lead from your true values, you will avoid leading from your hurts, disappointments, anger, or thirst for approval.

Before moving on, I'd like to summarize this chapter by recommending seven culture-creating ideas for pastors and leadership teams to communicate:

1. Define the look, feel, attitude, and spirit you want to see in your church.
2. Provide ongoing leadership training that communicates your values.
3. Give recognition and awards to those whose actions are consistent with the culture you are creating.
4. Show tolerance for honest mistakes that don't violate your culture and zero tolerance for those that do.
5. Use slogans, affirmations, and visuals (such as our values wheel) that inspire commitment to the culture of your organization.
6. When hiring staff, establish high criteria and a screening process for the purpose of evaluating if the person fits in the culture you are creating. (For more on this, see Strategy #3 on corporate competence.)
7. Talk in leadership settings about other churches that model specific elements of the culture you want to create.

At Champions Centre, our seven values of commitment, excellence, leadership, life, relevance, team, and wisdom are continually emphasized and communicated. Like the carefully designed culture of Disney, it's important to remember that you can't expect people in your church to know your

MVs or contribute to your preferred church culture without hearing it explained and seeing its evidence throughout the church. It should go beyond a piece of paper and be visible in the way the organization functions.

If you haven't already done so, I encourage you to set aside time to write down your Mission Statement, Statement of Faith, Vision Statement, Core Values, and Methods of Ministry that are relevant to your church's calling. Once the vision is clear, you will be surprised at how easily your church staff and volunteers are able to use the blueprint of your culture by design.

5

Establish a Life-Giving Platform

Over the years, we have put our efforts and energy into giving every church attendee an uplifting and spiritually inspiring experience every week. We have kept the Scripture from 2 Corinthians 3:6 as a guideline for the tone and launching pad of our messages. It reads: "He has made us competent as ministers of a new covenant—not of the letter but of the Spirit; for the letter kills, but the Spirit gives life." We want to give life, not death, through every endeavor we set out to do.

Consequently, a lot of thought and preparation goes into our services although they feel informal. At the Champions Centre, our staff knows that Sunday is the main event. It's the day of the week for which our team exists. Everything else we do is secondary to Sunday.

We refer to Sunday as "Game Day." In fact, we have derived slogans and volunteer campaigns from this. One campaign was a month-long series with the slogan, "Get out of the bleachers, and get into the game."

Our children's ministry team has a Game-Day checklist, where they mark off certain goals on a form to "keep score." At the end of the day, the question they ask is, "Did we win the game today?" Sometimes the answer is a resounding "YES!" and sometimes the scorecard gives us a chance to come back the next week and do things better. But the idea that Sunday is Game Day—the main event—is one that our ministry teams understand and embrace.

We are playing for the souls and lives of people, and it is too important to not recognize the value of a life-giving platform. Because our mission is to equip people to live successful lives, we don't want them to miss out on what we have ready to share with them. To inspire people to attend weekly and support the mission of the church, we know we must do this one thing well, so we, as staff and leaders, strive to make the Sunday services an excellent experience for all. Game Day is our oasis of faith, hope, and encouragement in a busy and challenging world.

➤ "Success Begins on Sunday"

I still remember well the moment in 1989 when my wife, Sheila, and I pulled the ministry theme out of our hearts that "Success Begins on Sunday." Since that time, churches have used that phrase across the nation and the world. For us, it was more than a catchy phrase; it was a theme we had sought as a way of saying to our community that real and lasting success begins by putting God first in our lives.

The Word clearly teaches us how to have successful lives. Jesus said to seek God's kingdom and

His righteousness first, and then all that we need will be added to us (See Matthew 6:33). The message is clear: if we want success in our lives, we must put first things first, which is to seek God and love Him with our whole heart.

When we began telling our community that success begins on Sunday on billboards, TV, and radio, we became even more committed to equipping people to live successful Christian lives.

Without a doubt, nothing is as important to the growth and health of the church as its church services. Interestingly enough, not all church leadership teams recognize the potential impact that a Sunday service can have on an individual's life, and many teams put far too little effort into that main weekly service.

The worst thing a pastor can do is be unsure of his goals for a church service. Uncertainty will lead to inconsistency, which will result in the deterioration of the quality of a service. Most good leaders instinctively know what they want to achieve in a service, but every pastor can benefit from looking at a list of potential service targets.

➤ Game-Day Targets

Here's the list I created to help me communicate what end results I wanted to see from our Sunday services. I gave this list of goals for a church service to our Sunday volunteer team:

- Life and energy
- Encouragement
- Sincerity
- Fun and laughter

- Good flow with smooth transitions
- Warmth and love
- Participative praise
- Heartfelt worship
- Cheerful giving
- Inspired learning
- People connections
- Life change
- Real decisions to follow Christ

The platform (singers, teachers, musicians) ministry is not more important than other ministries, but it *is* the most visible, and that makes it the greatest point of influence in the church. For that reason, I want every person who serves in this public point of reference to exude the energy and sincerity of the goals that I have established for the service.

Church buildings are designed for people's attention to be drawn to and focused on the platform. From the moment attendees arrive to the time they leave, the majority of their time will be spent looking at the platform. That is why everyone who participates in leading the service, from the singers to those making announcements, should be well versed in the MVs of the church and the service goals, so that they exude the same enthusiasm and relevancy that we have established as a value to our church.

One reason this is so important is that whatever happens on the platform can be either something that people have to overcome or something that helps them to overcome. In other words, if we do something that contradicts our teaching by speaking negative words of fear instead of positive words of faith, people will have to overcome our presentation in order to see God as the One who will meet their needs. But if we come ready to share the good news of His provision in everything that is said, done, or sung on the platform, people will be infused with confidence in God and trust Him for their needs.

The platform can make it harder to praise and worship God or easier to praise and worship God. When song leaders are more aware of their own performance than of the presence of God, they can make it difficult for others to focus attention on true worship.

The platform can tear down or build up. I have heard countless stories of people who have attended churches only to leave feeling more terrified of the future than when they woke up that morning. Spending time in the presence of God and sharing with His people should be an invigorating and faith-building experience.

The platform can bless people, give people hope, and grow people's faith. Of course, we want people to be blessed by what they see and hear at church. We live in an emotionally charged, burdened-down society that needs life-giving ministry. I don't think we have to lay hands on everyone to give life. If a platform is full of generous gestures, plenty of smiles, and encouragement, it will. The song, the scriptures read, even the offering time can bless people and build faith. The message from the platform can give life to those who are in the auditorium.

The message from the platform can be relevant or irrelevant to people's everyday lives. My teaching and preaching style could best be described simply as practical and relevant to life today. I'm not a fiery evangelist, so I'm often amazed at the numerous, first-time decisions that are made weekly in our church. I'm convinced that many people come to know the Lord at our church because they see salvation as a decision that leads to a better life here on earth, as well as an eternal future in heaven.

Oftentimes, churches try to get people's attention by talking about eternity when these same individuals just want to know how to make it through the week. Once people realize that God is interested in their everyday lives, and that a church can help them with daily issues and the complexities of modern life, they are more ready and willing to deal with the issue of eternity.

This message of abundant life "now" is completely opposite of the messages I heard as a child. A few decades ago, it seemed that preachers focused on teaching only about the afterlife. But I find that adults in this generation, as I suspect previous ones would have, are more willing to deal with their need for salvation once they realize that God is interested in their lives now.

Many more people will accept Jesus as their Lord if they hear a message that is relevant to their everyday lives. Our generation is not motivated by preaching that tells them what they *should do* or *should not do*.

People respond well to preaching that equips them with practical knowledge on *how* to do what they already know they *should* do. The "how to" lessons give us something we can apply in the here and now, and they empower us to experience positive life changes right where we are.

▶ Simplify the Platform Message

For the purpose of training our service teams, I have analyzed the components that create a life-giving platform (LGP) for our services. First of all, such a platform must have a refreshingly simple theme that is carried throughout the service.

A clear purpose for the service keeps the message from being all over the theology map and from answering questions that nobody is asking. An LGP focuses on providing consistently fresh messages that build, inspire, and equip the people to live the abundant life that Christ came to give us.

Pastors who focus on keeping their LGP messages simple will have a greater effect on their listeners. It takes more effort to keep a message simple and relevant, and it will certainly not get the applause of theologians who dismiss simple, clear communication as shallow. But Sunday morning is not the time to try to prove anything theological.

Sunday services are not the places to defend anything or build a case for something; they are simply a time to teach people how the gospel is relevant. People are looking for a truth that is applicable to their lives *today*. They need encouragement, motivation, and inspiration that God is on their side, that they are called to be champions in life, and that He is the answer. They need practical knowledge that can help them in their relationships at home, at work, and with their friends and family.

It has been said that the difference in educators and communicators is that educators make simple things complex and communicators make complex things simple. Within the context of local church leadership, we have the example of Christ who was "a life-giving spirit" (1 Corinthians 15:45) and whose words are "spirit" and "life" (John 6:63).

I have observed that great teaching, which brings a life-altering message, has key ingredients in it. Here's a checklist for pastors and teachers to consider when evaluating the life-giving substance in their message:

1. Is the message affirming?

    "You are the light of the world. A city on a hill cannot be hidden" (Matthew 5:14).

2. Is the message understandable?

    "If anyone has ears to hear, let him hear" (Mark 4:23).

3. Is the message digestible?

    "I gave you milk, not solid food, for you were not yet ready for it. Indeed, you are still not ready" (1 Corinthians 3:2).

4. Is the message directional?

    "When they had finished eating, Jesus said to Simon Peter, 'Simon son of John, do you truly love me more than these?'

    "'Yes, Lord,' he said, 'you know that I love you.'

    "Jesus said, 'Feed my lambs'" (John 21:15).

5. Is the message relatable?

> "To the weak I became weak, to win the weak. I have become all things to all men so that by all possible means I might save some" (1 Corinthians 9:22).

6. Is the message compatible?

> "I write to you, fathers, because you have known him who is from the beginning. I write to you, young men, because you have overcome the evil one. I write to you, dear children, because you have known the Father" (1 John 2:13).

7. Is it inspirational?

> "A student is not above his teacher, but everyone who is fully trained will be like his teacher" (Luke 6:40).

As I said earlier, I've found that simple themes and helpful messages are appreciated much more than complex ones. Contrary to common thought, when it comes to communication, *simple* is not easier and *complex* is not more difficult.

It takes much less effort to put together a sermon with information than it does to prepare a presentation. Creatively presenting information will mean you provide less information but you present it in such a way that people remember it and can apply it. This simplification is what transforms information into a life-giving form of communication.

> The Life-Giving Platform Should Be Affirmative

Besides being simple, the LGP should also be affirming in nature.

Jesus asked His disciples, "Who do people say I am?" (Mark 8:27). In other words, He was asking, "What's My reputation?" For the local church, that same question can benefit us in evaluating how well we are communicating to the people who live in our own community.

Our reputation doesn't necessarily reflect who we really are, but it is people's perception of us. It is important that the message we preach is also the one we practice. The message we teach should be a reflection of who we actually are because people hear about our reputations in the community before they hear our platform messages. We should be known as people who affirm others everywhere we go—not just at church.

A religious spirit demoralizes humanity, lowers morale, and weakens the spirit, confidence, and courage of a person. Jesus, on the other hand, affirmed people. He told His followers:

- You are the light of the world (Matthew 5:14).
- You should not spend one day in worry (see Matthew 6:34).
- Speak to the mountains in your life (see Mark 11:23).
- Do not let your hearts be troubled (John 14:1).
- My yoke is easy; my burden is light (Matthew 11:30).

When terrorists attacked the United States in September 2001, many pastors immediately changed their platform message to one of end-time theology or biblical prophecy and missed the opportunity to impart courage and lift people's spirits in one of our nation's darkest hours. People flooded their local churches for several weeks following the attack, hoping to find stable ground on which they could stand, but once their fears subsided so did their church attendance. Fear is not a lasting motivation to keep people in church, but affirmation is something people are always seeking.

Some preachers seem to believe that they have a mandate to declare and expound on man's sin, week in and week out. They imagine God is holding them responsible for shaming people into repentance. This unhealthy perspective causes them to constantly emphasize man's sense of guilt and low self-esteem. They perpetuate a cycle of sin, guilt, shame, and hopelessness that leads to more sin, more guilt, more shame, and more hopelessness.

I've found that most people already know they are sinners and have a high awareness of their unrighteousness. What they don't know and desperately need to hear is that they are greatly loved by God. People need to consistently be reminded that God doesn't want to put them *in shame;* He wants to release them *from shame.* A life-giving platform provides hope by affirming the value of every person's life and the redemption that is available to every believer. Rather than reminding people of their sins, the LGP will remind them of the hope and forgiveness that is in Christ. People who are affirmed are inspired to do better, rather than resigned to do worse.

➤ Avoid Issue-Oriented Messages

The LGP can be hindered when a leader's focus is on irritating issues and controversy. A message that is full of life is not issue oriented—it has no ax to grind.

As long as there are people on earth there will be issues. People have issues. An LGP can have a position on issues without being issues-oriented. Remember the issues that bombarded Jesus:

- Why do your disciples eat grain on the Sabbath? (see Matthew 12:2-4).
- This woman married seven brothers; who will be her husband in heaven? (see Matthew 22:25–28).
- Do we pay taxes or tithe? (See Matthew 22:15–22).

Jesus knew about these issues and had a position on the issues, but He did not allow issues to take over His platform. The church platform is not a place to settle the issues of the world, but it is a place to heal the hearts of individuals. Jesus did not answer the many questions asking him to take a position on issues. Instead, He stayed with His message, which further frustrated the issue-oriented people of His day.

A pastor must avoid letting his own struggles with people who are not serving, helping, worshipping, giving, or cooperating affect his life-giving message or keep it from flowing on the platform. The worst thing a pastor can do is preach his problems. Solve the problems and deal with the issues during the week, but preach a life-giving message from the platform on Sunday.

The best part of an LGP is that it motivates people. And motivation is not manipulation. It's not trickery or tactics to control people. We all know what needs to be done, but we may simply lack the motivation to do it.

I remember hearing the story of the wealthy businessman who threw a spectacular party and invited many guests. After filling the pool with small sharks and barracuda, he announced that anyone who would be brave enough to swim the length of the pool would receive their choice of a new home, a trip around the world, or a top position in his company.

He barely got the words out when he heard a splash. Within seconds, a guy swam the length of the pool and stood dripping wet on the other end. When the shocked businessman asked what he wanted as his prize, the wet swimmer said, still breathing heavily, "I want to know the name of the guy who pushed me in the pool!"

The LGP provides that *push* people need to face life courageously. An LGP tells people to stand strong in their faith and not lose heart!

➤ Guidelines for Choosing a Platform Team

On a life-giving platform, a person's expressions, enthusiasm, and authenticity always rate higher than talent. Enthusiasm comes from Greek words *En theos* or "in God," meaning "full of God." When a person shows enthusiasm, expression, and authenticity on the platform, he or she gives life to a congregation.

As a leader, it is important to guard against the platform becoming a place to showcase talent rather than a place of authentic, passionate worship. The LGP is a place for people with an authentic love for God and enthusiasm to praise Him. These people are able to sing without any reservation or timidity from a fully devoted and passionate heart.

One of our college students went to another church to intern there for the summer. After returning home, he expressed how different the concept of worship was in the church he had visited. He explained that the music consisted of two congregational songs and three specials as their worship service. In a culture like that, talent will always be seen as the most important thing.

Even if everyone, including the leader, says it's not talent that is the motivator there, it is. The only natural result of displaying so many solos and specials is to end up with a church that assumes the platform is a place to display talent and not a place to worship God.

The congregation will assume that playing an instrument or liking to sing is the only criteria for being on the platform. The result is a talented but sterile platform.

The Hillsong Church in Sydney, Australia, is a great example of an enthusiastic and authentic platform of people who sincerely want to worship and glorify God, not their own talent. The Praise and Worship team is obviously talented, but it's not just their talent that has made them one of the most listened to churches in the world. It's the authenticity with which they write and sing. Their heart for God can be felt in the music and is in the culture of their church.

The leadership of pastors Brian and Bobbie Houston and worship leader Darlene Zschech is not performance-oriented but is one that gives life. The focus is never on the performer but is directed to genuine worship and praise for God.

A sound LGP will cause people to lighten up. The presence of God will be evident, and there will be lots of smiling and genuine happiness. When Jesus said, "Come to me, all you who are weary and burdened, and I will give you rest" (Matthew 11:28), He was saying that His plan for life was not going to bring emotional heaviness. Instead, He was bringing us joy! His message is for us to enjoy life.

The Pike Place Fish Market in Seattle has become world famous. Just recently, however, it also has become an inspiration to corporate America because of the fun way the employees approach their work. A book titled *Fish* describes how the fish market employees have a good time and make it fun for everyone else, while selling more fish than any other market. Everyone knows that fish market work is not desirable, but the employees tapped into something when they started having fun. They sell more fish than anyone ever imagined they could, and now people come from all over the world to see them, not because of the fish, but because of the fun!

The Pike Place Fish Market has what I call a life-giving platform, which shows that this idea works in everyday life. Their Web site summarizes their LGP:

> A few years ago, we at Pike Place Fish Market committed ourselves to becoming "world famous." We've accomplished this—

not by spending any money on advertising (we've never spent a dime), but by being truly great with people. We interact with people with a strong desire to make a difference for them. We want to give each person the experience of having been served and appreciated, whether they buy fish or not. We love them.

At World Famous Pike Place Fish Market, we stand for the possibility of World Peace and Prosperity for all people. We believe that it's possible for a person to impact the way other people experience life. Through our work, we can improve the quality of life for others. We are committed to this belief. It's what we do.[1]

Buyers can get fish from other places, but they come to the Pike Place Fish Market for the experience, the fun, and the affirmation that the market personnel give to their customers. It's similar to a life-giving church that has enthusiastic worshippers sharing the platform.

Every time there's a life-giving celebration service, the experience will cause people to *lighten up* emotionally and spiritually.

Develop Corporate Competence

All churches have both a spiritual body and a corporate structure. Good management of the corporate structure or business side of the church is a key to the health of a church. The corporation performs practical functions just like any other business. Land and building acquisitions, budgets, liabilities, and employment are all a part of a healthy modern church.

My hesitation in writing this chapter is in not wanting to imply that I am a guru of corporate competence. And I'm certainly not implying that we have become a benchmark for anyone to aspire to. We have made our share of business blunders on the corporate side of our church. I've made some wrong administrative and staff decisions in my time as a pastor. But, I have never valued corporate competence any more than I do today.

If anything, my journey has made me more aware of the vital connection between corporate competence and the success of a church in its mission. I am able to alert other leaders to areas that will need careful attention in order to maintain a thriving church-culture.

Legal, Current, and Functional Concerns

More often than not, the bylaws of a church corporation will be legal, current, or functional, but rare is the church that has balance in all three areas. One reason for this is that most churches view bylaws like a holy document that should *never* be updated or changed. Yet, these same churches often update their day-to-day organization to function more effectively, even though it's in conflict with the *sacred writings* of the bylaws.

All is well until someone comes along and says, "Wait just a minute—that's not what the bylaws say," and sure enough everyone guilty of progress is found in contempt of the bylaws. This sort of dilemma is exactly why it is important to view the organizational bylaws as an ever-changing document that reflects the progress of the organization and facilitates its growth.

Articles of incorporation are filed with the state, and they should be lean in content in order to be less restrictive; they also should be kept updated whenever progress calls for it. Sometimes legal documents are outdated simply because no one is taking time to keep them up-to-date. Even when there are no anticipated problems with the way the bylaws read, it is a good practice to review them on a regular basis to see if any issues need to be addressed.

➤ Corporate Management Concerns

The corporate affairs of Champions Centre are managed by our executive staff and pastors council. The executive staff handles all the day-to-day operations including administrative, procedural, and staff issues. The council provides management guidance for budget setting, property acquisition, building programs, and debt retirement. Ideally, the council should be a combination of pastors and business leaders who, along with outside pastors, have a relationship with the senior pastor.

A smaller, new church should not rush to put in-house people on this team. It would be better to use outside, mature, proven leaders than to give a position like this to unknown, unproven, or novice individuals.

The council should always be pastor-led and pastor-appointed. One common and harmful misconception is that the church board exists to protect the church from the pastor, to police the pastor, to hold the pastor in check. This kind of mentality is why the average stay of a pastor at board-led churches is three years. When board members come to meetings and are adversarial to the pastor's vision, nothing positive can happen. Pastors have to be given the freedom and liberty to lead the church. If a church wants to grow, it must streamline its decision-making process to accommodate the visionary leadership of a pastor.

A pastor's responsibility to the council is to:

- Lead meetings.
- Assure minutes are taken.
- Provide the agenda.

- Provide finance reports (via the business manager).
- Be informative.
- Be open and desire advice.
- Lead the group to a consensus or look at other options.
- Be a Christlike leader.

A council member's responsibility to the pastor is to:

- Know and support the pastor's vision.
- Review financial reports.
- Make sure the pastor's family and personal needs are provided for.
- Assure the best salaries possible for pastors and staff in accordance with church size and growth.[1]
- Stay informed and educated on philosophies and concepts of growing churches.
- Keep church business confidential.
- Be resourceful.
- Be Christlike in attitude.

One of the most common and costly mistakes churches make is in the positioning of people. People in the wrong position will cause you and your church anxiety, frustration, financial loss, and lack of progress. Strange and sometimes destructive things happen when the wrong people end up with titles.

Flags go up anytime I hear of a person who *wants* a position, because typically that is the kind of person who will not handle it well. In my experience, these people may not come right out and ask for a title, but they let their ambition be

known in other ways. These people are not necessarily evil, but they can cause a lot of unnecessary
confusion and strife when they don't get their way.

The appetite that title seekers have for a position
is almost always disguised in terms such as, "I just
want to use my talents for God," or "The Lord
has told me that I am supposed to work at the
church." In fact, it's possible that individuals who
secretly want titles probably haven't admitted it to
themselves. Their sense of value is based on the
kind of recognition that a position or title can give
them, but they don't see it that way. Jesus gave us
the key to good people positioning when He told
His disciples, "If you want to be great, learn to
serve" (see Luke 22:26-28).

You will find the people with the greatest potential are focused on serving, on being the best they
can be right where they are. These people are not
distracted by concerns of status, titles, and positions. Their focus is on performance, not positions.

A clear indicator that a person is a candidate for
a promotion is when they serve without an agenda
for promotion. They are often surprised when
approached with the idea of being given a position
or a title. When people have no agenda for promotion you will find them serving joyfully and faith-
fully right where they are. They are not thinking, *I
hope the pastor notices me and asks me to be the
next. . . .* They may be eager to help in bigger
ways, but their foci are on making bigger contributions and not in getting promotions, titles, or positions.

Another important key when putting people in
positions is to know how they make decisions and
to be sure their thinking style is a match for the
role you are putting them in. There are profes-

sional career consultants who can evaluate your team members and potential applicants to give an assessment of where each person might thrive in your corporate structure.

One such test is Meyers-Briggs Type Indicator (MBTI). Assessments differentiate between people who work well as a leader or a taskmaster, people who work intuitively, or people who gather facts. All personality types have a place in the structure of the corporation, but it is important to help people serve in the right spot if you want the church to operate smoothly.

Another personality test that we have found to be tremendously helpful is the DISC Personality System.[2] The DISC shows whether people tend to be Dominant, Influential, Steady, or Competent. Combined with the MBTI, a lot of the guesswork can be taken out of the teambuilding efforts.

Some roles call for a strategic, contemplative, big-picture person. Other roles need a creative, out-of-the-box person. Another role may call for an individualized, sensitive person.

One thing's for sure—it's a lot easier to put people in a position than it is to remove them when it's not working. Putting people into positions or giving them titles and then having to remove them or taking away a title can result in hurt feelings, family involvement, congregational gossip, and department unrest.

Below are some things you can do to tip the odds in favor of a right choice when positioning people.

- Take your time when giving out titles.
- Do personality testing, values testing, and team placement testing *before* you invite

someone into a leadership position or hire someone.

- Position and hire people who make your vision their vision.
- Position and hire people who are low-maintenance.
- Position and hire people who are influencers of others (every staff leader must be able to attract volunteers, or you can't afford to hire them).
- Position and hire people who are competent in the role you are giving them.
- Hesitate to hire someone from within your church who is not first an outstanding volunteer.

Church staff must see their jobs as a ministry, not their ministry as jobs. Working at a church is not a typical job based on a person's skills and talent. Church work can only be done effectively when fueled by a passion of the heart.

When you are ready to hire for a position, look first at your volunteers to see if any of them have the qualifications and skills for the position you need to fill. If your volunteer team doesn't have someone who is qualified, you have two options:

1. Find a volunteer with the right profile who can learn the skills needed.
2. Look for someone outside your organization who has demonstrated a heart for the local church. If this option is the only choice you have, make sure you evaluate the candidate's work history, church background, and personality profile to determine if he or she is a potential fit.

➤ Staff Ownership and Responsibility

The "that's-not-my-job" mentality is stifling to any organization. Great organizations create job descriptions that provide the primary responsibilities of an employee, but not necessarily the limits of their involvement. In fact, today's premier companies have gone to flexible forms of organization that intentionally cause the lines to blur between individual responsibilities and raise the awareness that the company's success is every employee's responsibility. The piece of paper lying on the floor is not only the cleaning team's responsibility—it is everyone's responsibility.

Church staffs are notorious for taking on territorial, "that's-not-my-department" attitudes. However, team-minded people who assume responsibility for the overall success, reputation, and growth of the church create healthy churches.

It's common for our church staff to be involved with events outside their own job responsibilities. For example,

- Youth leaders help with children's camp.
- The children's pastor oversees a youth mission trip.
- The business administrator leads a small group.

All teams are involved in the mission of the church to make sure our conferences and special events are a success.

When hiring, ask yourself, "Is this person a fit on our team?" The question you want to consider when bringing someone in from the outside is whether or not the person will fit into the church culture.

I have seen pastors hire very talented individuals and within months both the pastor and the new staff member are unhappy. The reason is most often from a clash of church culture. One person may prefer traditional approaches while the other is looking for innovation. It isn't a matter of one person being right and the other wrong; it is simply a difference in management style. Most of this can be avoided by asking the right questions early in the process.

I first learned the value of team culture when my daughter Jodi was being recruited to play college basketball. After a coach verified Jodi's talent and ability on the court, the next thing he analyzed was how well she *fit* with the program. In basketball, coaches know what *style* of game they want to play, and they recruit players who play that style of game. A player can be a great talent but not a fit for the program. We learned to appreciate that way of thinking beyond the individual style and focusing on the game, and it helped us tremendously when it came time to decide on the right place for Jodi to be a student-athlete.

Interestingly enough, many pastors blunder past the "Is-it-a-fit?" question because they are excited about a person's likeability, musical talent, leadership skills, or management experience, while ignoring whether or not the person will enjoy working with the existing team and the leadership style that is already in place.

The staff team in a church must be in step with the pastor's approach and style of ministry. Some pastors are hands-on and relational in their approach to staff and ministry. These pastors will want to know the minute details of every department and every aspect of the staff member's work and decision-making processes. Other pastors will delegate authority to ministry and staff, preferring to receive written general reports each month.

A staff member who has a need for relational ministry style is not going to be happy for very long. And a staff member who has a highly individualistic style is going to be uncomfortable with a pastor who wants to micromanage his team. The point is not that there is a right way and wrong way to manage a church staff; it's a matter of style and personality, and the senior pastor is the one who should dictate this in his choice of staff and leaders by choosing people who match his style.

➤ Staff and Leadership Transitions

One of leadership's greatest challenges is skillfully facilitating and leading staff transitions. Church leaders are often so afraid of how staff changes may affect the church that they try to avoid them. Settle in your heart that part of any organization's growth is connected to good transitions and then get on with it. All healthy, growing churches have their share of staff changes; most on a frequent basis. Here are some suggestions for a senior pastor who needs to lead staff transitions.

The first way to prepare staff for smooth personnel changes is to frequently talk about transitions *before* you are facing one. Tell your staff that they can and should expect staff changes to happen without creating a hostile working environment where everyone is paranoid about who is leaving next. Help everyone to embrace the reality that change is an essential part of progress. Create a change-friendly culture that recognizes your structure as one of strength.

In our staff assessments, we use personality, value, and skill testing to help us place people from the beginning in the right fit. However, sometimes it is necessary to move good people from a place of weakness and put them in a place of strength. This may mean moving people from one role or position on the staff to another—to a better fit. Sometimes it means releasing them altogether.

Recognize that there are different reasons for staff moves, and communicate to your staff and team that under most circumstances, a staff change is the result of positive growth and progress for the church. Here are some common reasons for staff changes in the church:

- A person who is not flourishing in one role is moving to another that is a better fit.
- A new position has opened up, and a staff member in one job role is being promoted to another.
- A staff member who has done his or her job well in the past is leaving.
- The church has grown and so has the need for increased capacity in a role, but the person is unable to handle the increased responsibilities.
- Personal choices and life situations can precipitate changes in staff.

It is helpful if you guide the church staff to understand that commitment to the church should never be based on *working* at the church. Being called to and committed to a church is the only right reason for being a staff member of a church.

I recently heard from a pastor friend who asked a staff member if he would attend their church if he didn't work there. The staff member said, "Honestly, no." The pastor responded by telling him to find a new church and a new job. That was the right thing to do. Anyone who works for a church where he or she does not have a call to serve is merely a hireling and should not be part of the leadership team or church staff because they are not there for the right reasons.

The second way to facilitate leadership changes is to keep from sitting on the sidelines when it is time to make a transition. Lead change; don't retreat from it.

In some situations, especially in larger churches, the senior pastor may not be directly involved in every transitional process. When dealing with support staff, others may lead the process, but the pastor should be the coach who is calling the plays. The pastor should conclude what he wants to see happen and lead accordingly.

If the pastor doesn't project a clear vision, the team will flounder and lose momentum in what they have come together to achieve. President Ronald Reagan once told this story about the consequence of such indecision. A mother took her son to a shoe cobbler to get some shoes made for him. When the cobbler asked whether he wanted round toes or square, he couldn't make up his mind. After a long delay, the cobbler said, "Come back in a few days, and I'll have them ready for you." When young man returned, the cobbler had made one shoe with a round toe and the other with a square toe. Obviously, indecision can cause you to get something you don't want.[3]

It is wise to provide written guidelines for positive transitions to the staff member before there is even a need to make transitions in your church. I close this chapter with some general guidelines that I have given to my key staff members. We make it a practice to review these kinds of ethical guidelines with all of our staff on an annual basis.

Transitions don't have to be negative; you can and should be positive in your dealings with church staff. Changes can be extremely positive. Pastors have to keep positive publicly and as a rule should not share their most sensitive feelings about a change that is inevitable. In other words, realize that how you feel is secondary to your responsibility to lead a positive transition.

Also, keep in mind that everyone who wants to initiate transition is not being rebellious or trying to control everyone else. The stress and division of transition in the local church is sometimes due to the insecurity of the senior pastor. If the senior pastor is insecure, his insecurities will keep him from creating guidelines and leading positive transitions.

On the other hand, although a pastor can facilitate a positive transition, the ultimate responsibility for positive transition rests on the individuals who are leaving or changing roles. When the person transitioning is committed to the strength and unity of the church, he or she will remain positive and optimistic toward every part of the transition. It's a sign of maturity when transitions occur gracefully and positively.

➤ General Guidelines for Pastors and Key Individuals Who Leave a Church Staff

1. Make the unity and strength of the church your highest priority. Consider it and pro-

tect it above personal issues or differences you may have with other staff or church leaders.

2. As soon as you have a recurring sense that you want to make a change, *go first* to your senior pastor or designated overseer.

3. Realize that the senior pastor works for the church, and all other staff members work for the senior pastor. Your responsibility is to honor the guidelines for transition according to the wishes of the senior pastor. (These may vary circumstantially.)

4. Expect nothing from the pastor or church you are leaving that has not been previously agreed to in writing.

5. Don't communicate your plans with church members unless the pastor has released you to, and make sure you let him decide when, how, and with whom it is communicated.

6. Aspiring staff pastors should never start a church or accept a position in a church in the same city without the blessing of the senior pastor. Relocating to a new position should only be done if the new church location is a one-hour drive away, or more.

7. Staff pastors who decide to start their own church should not allow anyone to go with them unless the senior pastor suggests sending a team.

Create a Culture that Values Men and Women

God didn't give dominion only to *man;* He created men and women to rule over the earth together. Genesis gives a clear record of God's intention for equality to exist between His sons and daughters:

> God said, "Let us make man in our image, in our likeness, and let them rule . . . ." So God created man in his own image, in the image of God he created him; male and female he created them. God blessed them and said to them, "Be fruitful and increase in number; fill the earth and subdue it . . . ." He created them male and female and blessed them. And when they were created, he called them "man" (Genesis 1:26–28; 5:2).

Notice the above Scripture says that God blessed them, spoke to them, and called both of them "man". The idea conveyed in this Scripture is that the highest level of authority is in the unity of man and woman. When God used the term *man,* He was not just a referring to the masculine gender but also to the feminine gender. In the very nature of life, men and women are partners. The success of one is dependent on the success of the other. God didn't give Adam dominion—He gave *them* dominion. God didn't create him to rule—He created *them* to rule.

I am convinced that one of the keys to the health and growth of our church has been our recognition of men and women whom God has appointed as teammates. Both men and women have a responsibility to be involved in leading the church.

If either men or women become passive in the work of the church, the pendulum swings away from "them," a place of balance. In order to maintain a healthy atmosphere, both men and women must stay positive, encouraging, and assertive. Both must take ownership of the needs of the church. Neither can be hesitant or back away. Sometimes the men retreat from helping; sometimes the women retreat, but in a healthy church neither men nor women back away from the corporate responsibility to build one another in the faith. Men and women working together offer balance in ministry.

➤ Involve Men and Women on Planning Teams

Cognitive scientists have proven that men and women respond differently to life choices. In fact, when men are asked to make a quick decision, they typically use the left side of their brains, which defines rules such as math formulas and grammar. Women, on the other hand, tend to use their right brain, where creative ideas are formed, before engaging the rules stored in the left side of the brain. This helps to explain why a team comprised of all men would approach circumstances, evaluate decisions and actions, and respond to situations differently than a team that is comprised of all women.

There are certain times in the year when our church schedules an event that is just for women or just for men. But looking at the difference in how our events run also illustrates why healthy church teams need to have both men and women on them.

To illustrate this point, think about the difference in "men only" and "women only" church events. At our annual women's Oxygen Conference, one of the greatest things about the conference is the attention my wife Sheila brings to having "girl" fun before and after the event. But can you imagine a men's conference where the guys decide to have a pajama party at the end of one of the evening's sessions? It just wouldn't happen. The guys want a conference where the speaker speaks, they take notes, and then they go home afterwards. No home and garden shows, no pajama parties, no matching shirts, and no pink platforms! Men want to cut to the chase, accomplish the mission, and go home. The women's conference, on the other hand, is as much about what happens before and after the speakers as it is about the message that is delivered from the podium.

It wouldn't work for only men or only women to plan events intended for the entire church body to enjoy together. (The only ministry that should be all women or all men is the women's and men's ministries.) If a church team has an unhealthy balance in gender representation, it will plan events and make decisions that meet the needs of only one group of people.

Churches where a disproportionate number of women are involved in the children and youth ministries, adult education, etc., are also going to see that same percentage of more women than men in the pews on Sunday morning. Churches that have vastly more men, or all men, in the volunteer and staff ranks can almost guarantee that they are not a growing church.

The saying, "If Momma ain't happy, ain't nobody happy," will lead to Momma not wanting to come to church at all because it is not meeting her needs. And if Momma doesn't go to church, it is unlikely that the rest of the family, husband included, is going to go without her.

Think about it. You can probably name many married women who come to church even though their husbands are unsaved or do not attend for one reason or another. But how many men can you name who have wives at home on Sunday while they attend with their children? Not too many. The point is that the needs of both men and women must be addressed to create a healthy atmosphere in the church, and the only way that will truly happen is to have balanced teams where men and women serve side by side in the area of their gifting.

And that leads to another point. While men and women are going to naturally be drawn in higher numbers to certain areas of ministry, there should be overall *balance* in every department. For example, you might expect to see more women involved in the infant and toddler classrooms and more men attracted to the security department. But usher and greeter teams, parking lot ministries, bookstore teams, and prayer partners should be gender-balanced. If they are not, you may want to take a look at policies or practices that are causing an imbalance.

In Romans 16, Paul commends the contribution of his teammates to the progress and growth of the ministry. Of those named, many of them are women, revealing the active role both men and women took in building the early church.

We have a responsibility to create a culture that honors, loves, and celebrates masculinity and femininity.

The following is a description of the culture we endeavor to create:

1. *Create a gender-friendly culture.*

    A gender-friendly culture has an abundant appreciation and high value for both men and women. In a healthy church, you should be able to look around and see happy men and women "thriving" side by side.

    Have you ever noticed that in some churches there are few (if any) confident, ambitious, fully alive women? Even if they outnumber the men, they usually have a *tired* look about them. Have you also noticed that in some churches the men seem *bored* with being there? As you look around, do you see men who appear to have shut down mentally and emotionally? These same men are much more alive at work and play, but the church service lacks stimulation for the masculine mind.

On the other hand, a gender-friendly church culture attracts, awakens, and inspires men and women who are hungry to be fully alive. Healthy churches do a good job of identifying and connecting with the needs and interests of both women and men. In these churches, the tired women and bored men are the exception, not the rule. Instead there's energy and interest not found in churches where women are oppressed or where men are noticeably out-numbered.

2. *Inspire a leadership culture where the absence of masculinity or femininity is detected and countered.*

Although proactive thinking begins with the church at large being attractive to both men and women, the leadership team should counter any old thinking that stereotypes some ministries as being for women and some as being for men. For example, women may gravitate more quickly to children's ministry than men, but attentive leadership teams will make a point to get men involved with the chil-dren, which will attract more men to par-ticipate.

The music ministry also should be bal-anced with men and women participating. It may require intentional recruitment and effort to attract male vocalists, but it is equally challenging to attract female musi-cians. We have a female guitar player and a female bass player in our band, and it is a fantastic variation from the norm. People love to see stereotypes countered.

Seeing men and women serving in positions that are normally dominated by the opposite gender will breed the thought that it is good for men and women to be involved together everywhere in the church. In our children's ministry, we have an equal number of men in team leadership roles as we have women.

3. *Encourage a culture where masculinity and femininity are both worn like a badge of honor.*

When we break down old gender stereotypes, we don't want a culture that dilutes male and female pride. When both men and women are celebrated, their unique strengths emerge.

Our congregation loves the good-natured bantering between the sexes that happens when we promote a women's conference (no men allowed!) or an "estrogen-free" men's event. That good-natured fun adds fuel to the fires of gender pride that encourages both sexes to be proud of being the gender God created them to be.

At our women's Oxygen Conference, Sheila adds teenagers into the mix and makes it an event for girls of all ages. It's amazing how much fun they all have together. But beyond the fun, what I've noticed most is how they all emerge with their badge of honor fully shined and visible. It's as if they have a new awareness and affirmation of how great it is to be a woman. What a great teaching time this is for our young girls, as they see how their role in the church is valued and their leadership in the church for the future is encouraged.

I saw a movie recently called *Raising Helen*. In the movie, the main character is a single woman left as guardian of her sister's children when her sister and brother-in-law die in a car accident. While her life is being turned inside-out due to the circumstances, she enrolls the children in a private Christian school and in the process meets the (single) pastor. The two of them fall in love.

The pastor's character is refreshingly confident in himself as a man. The movie shows him involved in recreational sports, having a social life, and being attracted to the female character. In one particular scene, after she has turned down his invitations to date, he smiles at her and just to let her know his confidence is not shaken he says, "I'm a sexy man of God, and I know it!" It was a great movie moment for Christian men who sometimes need to be reminded to proudly wear their masculine badge of honor.

4. *Champion a culture that identifies positions in ministry by the heart of a person, not by his or her gender.*

The Word says simply: "There is neither Jew nor Greek, slave nor free, male nor female, for you are all one in Christ Jesus" (Galatians 3:28). This observation is not a denial of gender differences, but it is talking about how preferential treatment based on gender should not be a part of the culture of the house of God.

When I was looking for a music pastor, I wasn't looking for a man or a woman. I was looking for someone with the heart to lead our church in the celebration of praise and worship. My longest serving personal assistant (PA) to date was a man. I remember other pastors saying to me that they liked that, and they were looking for a man to put in that position. However, I didn't choose my PA because he was a man; I chose him because he had the right heart and was the right person for the role. The interesting thing is that my current PA (his replacement) is a woman! She also has the right heart and is the correct person for the role. When the gender package is an issue, the possibilities are limited. When it is not an issue, you double the possibilities.

In the story of Israel's deliverance from Sisera's army (See Judges 5–6) two women, Deborah and Jael, led the way. The leadership and courage they provided inspired and liberated their nation. The right person for the roles you need to fill may be in a gender package that is causing you to not recognize them. You could be overlooking God's answer to your prayer and not realizing that they are right in front of you.

5. *Applaud a culture that recognizes the pastor's wife as a leader and influencer in the life of the church.*

Anything less than this truth is denial and an unrealistic idea of whose influence is affecting the church. A pastor's wife is his first lady, the neck that turns his head. My recommendation is that her amazing potential to be a positive influence should be acknowledged and encouraged rather than ignored. If she has no "official" role in an organizational flow chart, it should not automatically be assumed that she has no part to play in the operation and growth of the church.

At the very minimum, a pastor's wife provides a unique partnership to her husband that no elders, board, or staff can provide. That partnership is inseparable from his leadership. Meaning if her partnership and marriage with him is healthy, he will be a better and more balanced leader. His approach to leadership will have the added perspective that *only* a wife can provide.

I recall seeing a book that asked the question: "When God speaks, why does He sound so much like my wife?" Most men will agree (perhaps secretly) that when a wife voices her opinion (and my wife has no trouble doing that), most men wonder why they didn't think of that before. Without her perspective, his blind spots remain.

I think most people underestimate the powerful potential the presence of the pastor's wife offers the church family. Her femininity and strength can provide affirmation to the women of the church. When she carries herself with ease in her fast-paced life, she gives others courage to do the same. When she greets them and smiles at them, she gives them assurance.

One woman who attends our church said to me, "I love your teaching, but your wife

by design or default?

is a huge part of my being in this church."
What's amazing is this woman doesn't have
a one-on-one friendship with Sheila.
However, Sheila's *presence* in the life of our
church has obviously meant a lot to her.
Even if it's subtle to most eyes, an up-close
observation will locate a correlation
between a healthy church and a healthy
couple leading it.

6. *Acknowledge that the church of the future
   is a church led by men and women.*

   Yesterday's church was a church dominated by male leadership. It was merely a
reflection of the male-dominated society
rather than a biblical order intended to
remain throughout generations of time. The
church of this generation will also be a
reflection of society as it is led by both men
and women.

   In recent decades, the increase in the percentage of women in the workforce has
been overwhelming. *Business Week Online*
(February 2000) compared the changes that
occurred between 1950 and the year 2000
in the United States female workforce:

- Female architects nearly quadrupled, to
  16 percent of the field.
- Female economists nearly tripled, to 51
  percent.
- Female pharmacists increased sixfold, to
  49 percent.
- Female lawyers went up sevenfold, to 29
  percent.
- Women now comprise 50 percent of all
  journalists.[1]

According to the White House,[2] in 1999 about 60 percent of females 16 years of age and older were in the workforce, up from 20 percent at the turn of the twentieth century.

What does this trend mean to the church? It means our generation expects women to be active in the life of the church. And why shouldn't they be? The church should be their place of greatest strength; a place where they share dominion—men and women partnering together to build God's kingdom on earth. The church of the future is full of the joy encouraged by like-mindedness and oneness in spirit and purpose.

> "Then make my joy complete by being like-minded, having the same love, being one in spirit and purpose" (Philippians 2:2).

by design or default?

8

Create a Team Church Culture

In 2005, my daughter Jodi was in her senior year at Western Washington University, and she enjoyed playing on a basketball team that had a 19–2 record. They were tied for first place in their conference. Then the unthinkable happened. One Saturday night, they journeyed to Humboldt University to play a team that was in *last* place, and Western lost the game!

The upset left everyone wondering what had happened. Everyone, that is, except Jodi's team. They knew what had happened and vowed in the late night meeting following the game to not let it happen again. It was simple: they had not played *together;* they had not played like a team. The absence of a team spirit and failure to function like a team had greatly reduced their effectiveness.

What's true in sports and business is also true in church life. The entire concept of church is based on teamwork. "Doing church" as a team is not a new concept. In fact, the first thing Jesus did when He began His earthly ministry was recruit a team.

There are few things more honoring to God than His people serving and working together, "being likeminded, having the same love, being one in spirit and purpose" (Philippians 2:2). Without a doubt, this verse expresses the culture in which God intended the church to function.

An orchestra is a group of people united in their love for music who gather for the purpose of performing a symphony. In a similar way, team church is a group of people who are united around a mutual love for God and His kingdom purpose. Many who attend a church will continue to live disconnected lives until they experience the joy and personal fulfillment that comes from being active and involved.

Modern trends are for people to withdraw into isolation via computers and television. But disconnected lives leave people unfulfilled and hungry for community. That is where the church has a great opportunity to bring people into community and enhance their lives.

There was a term used in the late '90s that described society's retreat from connectedness due to modern technology. That term was *nesting*. People began spending more and more time at home, isolated and out of relationship with one another. Outside of jobs, it appeared as if American culture was shifting from neighborhood and community into a place where people could not give you the names of the people living next door.

But there has been a new, subtle shift toward connecting once again. The term sociologists now use is *cocooning*. People are spending more time in their homes, it's true, but they are creating environments where instead of isolating themselves, they are building friendships and connections again, this time in their homes. More and more people are creating entertainment rooms, backyard retreats, and living spaces that are larger than before in order to host gatherings and parties. In the '50s and '60s, people met each other at local drive-ins, malt shops, and barbershops. In the '70s and '80s, it was the movie theaters and entertainment venues that attracted groups of people to get together. The '90s saw a retreat from it all, with declining statistics for most arenas outside of the movie theaters, but now we are seeing a reemergence of the need to connect.

▶ People Connect While Working Together

The church should recognize that people want to have connections with others. When building teams, the best way to grow them is for the leaders to recognize that the main goal should not be for the team to simply perform a function. The desire should be for the team leaders to help people connect with one another while they work at accomplishing a mutual goal.

Most immature leaders underestimate the dynamic of linking people together through teams. Instead, they recruit out of their *need* for people to do things for them, instead of recruiting people to help them get connected to the church in a greater way. Leaders need to recognize that their first responsibility should be to connect the team members so that they enjoy working together. Secondary to that should be rallying them around the needs of the church.

111

People who have relationships usually don't leave a church. It's when people become disconnected that they find a reason to leave. A person who comes and performs a duty without feeling connected to a team will eventually feel unappreciated.

A person who is part of a team dynamic will not see the duties performed as the main thing; rather they will see the duties as secondary to the relationships they have made in the process. It doesn't matter what the duties are; if there is a genuine team dynamic at work, people will flock to the team out of the unspoken desire they all have to be connected.

Focus on creating an interactive culture in and around church. People are drawn to friendly places. Coffee houses that merge with bookstores, such as Starbucks and Barnes & Noble, know their success is not about books and coffee; it's about building community among people who happen to like books and coffee. In the same way, friendly atmospheres are the frontline of creating a team church culture.

▶ Provide a Rally Point

Some atmospheres seem to *beg* for people to gather and interact. It is possible to create an atmosphere that will attract people of all ages. An atmosphere can be designed that advertises to all who enter it:

> This is a people-friendly zone. Come in, sit down, hang out . . . people love to gather here, so why not join them!

There are several components that create this team-centered atmosphere, but perhaps the most important one is to provide something for people to gather around. Some churches see this kind of expenditure as a waste of money, but nothing could be further from the truth. Anything will work: a coffee shop, bookstores, spacious lobbies, children's playgrounds, youth game rooms . . . anything that draws people together outside of the actual service time is a worthwhile investment. When you invest in peoples' relationships, you invest in the culture of a team church.

Wise church leaders will encourage people to leave the bleachers and get in the game. They will provide a clear path into the life of the church. They will inspire people out of isolation and into community, out of individualism and into the team church.

More and more Americans view churches as spiritual pit stops rather than church homes. We communicate by design the theme that church is not just a place to attend, but a community to belong to.

Unchurched people who start attending a church don't usually stay distant intentionally. Most often they are simply unaware of how to come into the community. That's where the next phase of team-building comes in.

> **Assimilation**

Visitors represent 100 percent of a church's growth potential. The question is how do we effectively transition people from being a visitor to being an active, serving part of the community?

In the book, *The Tipping Point,* author Malcolm Gladwell tells of a psychologist who did an experiment at Yale University to see if he could persuade a group of college students to get a tetanus shot. He divided them into groups and gave them a free booklet. The booklet explained the dangers of tetanus, the importance of inoculation, and the fact that the university was offering free tetanus shots at the campus health center.

Some students were given the "high-fear" version, complete with pictures, while other students were given the "low-fear" version. Those given the low-fear version were more convinced of the dangers and the importance of shots and were quicker to say they would get inoculated. However, one month later almost none of the students (3 percent) had actually gone to get a shot!

Then he redid the experiment and added a campus map with clear directions to the health center and the specific times shots would be given. Response increased to 28 percent! The students' main need was to know *how* to fit the tetanus shots into their lives. By adding maps, times, and directions, the brochure went from being an informative medical brochure to a practical guide to better health![1]

As we referred to earlier in the book, churches that experience growth have learned to shift their emphases from telling people *what* they should do to informing people *how* to do it. For example, rather than trying to convince people that they need to belong to the church, thriving churches focus on informing people *how* to join and get plugged in to the church. Rather than putting a lot of energy into telling people that they *should* give offerings, they focus on informing people *why* and *how* to give.

My wife Sheila drew our attention (mine and other staff leaders') **to roadblocks** that people experienced when coming to our church. We discovered three primary roadblocks hindering people from intergrating into our church.

1. **A Lack of Direction.**

   People need a roadmap. We designed a pathway of purpose for people to use as a roadmap. Churched or un-churched need to know where to go from where they are at now. Just as when you walk into a fitness center for the first time. You don't know how to use the equipment, you feel overwhelmed, you need direction. Our Pathway of Purpose provides a roadmap into the life of our church. See Chapter 8.

2. **A Lack of Information.**

   People need information. Assume people don't know anything about your church. Provide an information center where visitors can be encouraged to stop and ask questions. Secondly, provide a membership class that communicates your mission, methods and values.

3. **A Lack of Connectivity.**

   Isolation is the greatest enemy of community. Our Assimilation teams work at connecting people into the community of Champions Centre. Anyone who serves in Baptism Ministry, Information Centers, as Ushers, Greeters, and Altar Workers must understand the goal is to get people connected.

Until we discovered these roadblocks, we had thought of ourselves as one of the most user-friendly churches in town. We constantly encouraged people to attend membership class and join a ministry team or small group. However, we recognized the need to communicate a less cumbersome and clearer pathway for people to follow when moving from the position of a *believer* to the position of *belonging*.

We committed ourselves to create a clear and informative plan for transitioning from believing to belonging. As we committed ourselves to a more fluid assimilation into our church family, we experienced an obvious surge of growth in our church attendance and the number of people eager to assimilate into the core of our church. The difference was as though we had been in a position of having a five-lane highway with three lanes blocked, and we finally had removed the barriers.

➤ Show Visitors How to Get Involved

Sheila and I celebrated twenty-five years of marriage by touring Switzerland and Italy by train. The people there ride trains so much they assume everyone knows *how* to ride the trains. There is not much signage other than departure times and destinations. At the risk of sounding completely incompetent, we had to force information out of people after we had already made mistakes.

When asking where to board, we could get little more than a nodded head in the direction of the train or a rushed explanation (sometimes not in English), and still we boarded the wrong trains. At first, we were under the impression that all trains were the same and focused primarily on the train's destination.

We didn't realize that the Eurostar, the train we had paid extra to ride, was on a different schedule and its departure was every other hour. Again, no one bothered to inform us at the train stations or when checking our tickets. The other trains were not as nice and not air-conditioned like the Eurostar. It was frustrating because we couldn't seem to get the information we needed. Since we knew something wasn't right, we kept asking and finally, by the fourth ride, we had it all figured out.

When you have been attending church for a long time, it's easy to forget what it is like to be a first-time visitor. It is easy to overlook the informational needs people have when they attend a new church environment. We have discovered that visitors know a lot less than we would assume they know, both practically and spiritually. The same disorientation that Sheila and I felt when trying to board the Eurostar happens to visitors in churches every Sunday. People get up the nerve to attend but often end up confused and unsure of how to become a part of the church.

At Champions Centre, we have a four-step process called the Pathway of Purpose, which we use as a way of recognizing where people are in their relationships with the church. This helps our team to understand the assimilation process. It also helps our team move people along consistently until they become part of the church community.

We first initiate *contact*, which occurs through our special events, media, or when they visit our Sunday service. Then we offer a relational *connection* by inviting newcomers to a guest reception, making a follow-up call, or responding to a request on our visitor's record. Then *commitment* occurs when a person decides to belong and attends the Team 101 class. Full assimilation occurs through *community,* when a person is an active, functioning member of a ministry team or small group at our church.

For the individual who we are encouraging to progress toward community, we simply phrase the four steps in a way that personalizes the path. We remind our volunteers of this four-step process in the Joining the Team Class 101 and periodically with our congregation in order to remind everyone of the simple steps to the Pathway of Purpose.

People respond well when the map is clear. So here's how the four-step process would sound to you as a person in route to community. Our literature, staff members, volunteers, and church family would all communicate the same simple steps, like this:

- Make Contact. You have already done this if you're in attendance at church. One step down, three steps to go!
- Get Connected. If you are in attendance, but you haven't stopped by our guest center, come by and introduce yourself to us. We would love to meet you and explain the various small groups where you can meet people who share your interests.
- Be Committed. Getting planted in the house of God (see Psalm 92:13) is God's plan for every believer. It's the right choice for everyone who wants to grow in their faith. Sign up for our class called Joining the Team 101 when you're ready to volunteer with the rest of the team.

by design or default?

- Live in Community. Church is not just a place to attend—it's a community to which you belong. Within community you will experience ongoing fellowship and maturity of faith with people of all ages.

If people enroll in Joining the Team Class 101, they are encouraged when they see the Pathway of Purpose for the first time because they are already over halfway along their journey. They only have one more step to take to be in the *community*.

Commitment occurs upon completion of the class and is celebrated on confirmation Sunday in our service when we welcome the new members. It's exciting for them to realize they only have one more step to belonging, which is to join a ministry team and experience the joyful life in community with God's family.

Growth by Design

If you don't have an assimilation plan in place, I encourage you to use our four-step process to help you get started. The first step is to design a guest reception center, if you do not presently have one. If you have a guest center that isn't receiving much activity, take a new look at it and analyze what you could do to motivate more people to go there.

The primary goal is not just to give away information and welcome gifts. The primary goal is to capture information about your visitor and establish contact with the guest. If a visitor goes to the guest center, they should leave knowing at least one person and knowing that person is there to help them get acclimated and connected to the church.

If you have not already done so, define an assimilation plan such as our Pathway to Purpose with a specific starting point and arrival point. In other words, it may begin when a person responds to an opportunity like guest reception, salvation, or membership, and continue until they are on a ministry team.

Be sure that your leadership team understands the assimilation plan and communicates it to new contacts. The assimilation plan is the growth plan of the church and all of its ministries. The more effort the leadership team puts into assimilating people, the more visitors become members. When membership increases, volunteer teams grow. This, of course, is a main goal of staff leadership.

> Growing Teams that Grow the Church

Teams exist throughout society. The family unit is a team. In hospitals, medical teams carry out the mission of a successful surgery. In air travel, flight crews carry out the mission of a safe and successful journey. Team Boeing exists to build airplanes. Team Starbucks exists to make great coffee. Team Nordstrom exists to sell clothes. In the same way, Team Church exists to build God's house and increase God's kingdom. Teams succeed by being like-minded, being one in spirit and purpose. Team Church is no exception.

Remember the Titans is a movie that tells the true story of a high school football team in the state of Virginia and their first season as a racially integrated team. It highlights the conflicts of once segregated young men who are thrown together and challenged by their leader-coach Herman Boone (played by Denzel Washington) to become a team. As their unity grew, so did their commitment and pride. They showed it in the way they sang their theme song together: "We are the Titans—the mighty, mighty Titans." The Titans recognized their team identity in a way that superseded individual differences. They had a 13–0 season and won the championship.

Church leaders have a similar challenge as the Titans' coach, which is to help people recognize their team identity in a way that supersedes individual differences.

The church exists to inspire people to see themselves as the church—the mighty, mighty church. Jesus said that He would build the church (See Matthew 16:18). We exist to inspire people to join Christ in His mission of building the church (Matthew 16:18) by giving of their time and talents as volunteers.

So how do we grow a team of volunteers? The first key in growing teams that help grow the church is to *recognize that every person has a need to be a part of the church*. Churches have a tremendous resource in volunteers who *need* a place to give their time and talent. Here are some of the reasons why church members need to be on a team:

- When they volunteer, they feel good about themselves.
- When they volunteer, they feel connected to the mission of the church.
- When they volunteer, God blesses their lives.

- When they volunteer, they are less likely to drift away from the church community where God called them to be.
- When they volunteer, they experience the joy of using the gifts God gave them.
- When they volunteer, they experience a connection with their team.
- When they volunteer, they fulfill their purpose in life.

The second key in growing a team is *to not ask for volunteers just because you need help.* As strange as it seems, asking for help because you need it is usually counterproductive when team building.

You can usually ask for help on a one-time event basis without experiencing a negative kickback. But there is a much better, more effective approach to team building than soliciting help.

Need is everywhere. What people really want is to volunteer for something purposeful, which is a basis beyond being needed. People want to volunteer for something that gives them an opportunity to be a *blessing* to others. It's important that church leaders recognize this and develop a basis for recruiting volunteers that extends beyond a need and offers opportunity for people to use their gifts in a service to the Lord.

A church culture where everyone volunteers on the basis of need is a culture of low morale and low motivation. In this culture, volunteers serve grudgingly, as if they are doing church leaders a favor. To build great teams that build great churches, there are ten initiatives that can be incorporated into your plan.

> ## Ten Team Building Principles

1. *Share your vision and mission, over and over again.* When leaders want volunteers to have a long-term, fulfilling experience, they should communicate the cause and show people the value of their involvement as a volunteer by explaining the purpose and mission of the team.

2. *Share great stories.* Telling others about people who are already serving and how they have benefited from the efforts of the team is motivating and inspiring. Emphasize the ongoing positive relationships and the fun the team enjoys by working together. And share stories of team successes!

3. *Be a team that people want to belong to.* A team that has a positive energy, loves each other, is welcoming to new team members, and believes in its purpose will not have a hard time growing. This is why team leaders must protect the spirit of the team from negativity and lead the team in an ongoing, fresh commitment to its purpose.

4. *Get organized.* Life is busy, and people realize that it is also too short to volunteer on a team that is disorganized. Leaders can enhance the team experience by having a clear, well-organized approach to ministry. It sends a message to volunteers that you appreciate their time and will make good use of it by guaranteeing that all meetings and team functions are well-planned.

5. *Recognize that more people doing less is healthier than fewer people doing more.*

The most successful teams are ones that have many people each doing a small part for the team. There are people who are volunteer martyrs and relish the role of being the rescuer or hero of the ministry. But it is very unhealthy for them, and for the church, to allow people to build "fiefdoms" by always serving in a ministry and never being in adult services. They become disconnected, develop grudges, resent anyone not involved in "their" ministry area, and form unhealthy cliques of other people who feel as they do. The best way to prevent this is by having teams of people working together instead.

In our children's ministry, team members serve just once per month, although they are there for all services that day. The other three weeks, they are expected to be in adult services. Our children's pastor asks without reservation for them to give 110 percent effort on the week they are "on." She would not be able to do that if they were in the classrooms every week. And when you have this as your model, if a person leaves the team, it is not a catastrophe because they are just one small part of a big team.

6. *Recruit from your strength and joy, not from your problems and weaknesses.* The best recruiters are happy volunteers; this is why it is important to structure the work volunteers do and the climate in which they work so that they have a positive experience. When that happens, they become informal recruiters by telling others how rewarding it is to be on the team.

7. *Teach team leaders that their most important role is connecting with their team members.* While certainly we need volunteers to perform their functions as team members, the reality is that it is the connectedness of people working with each other that helps a church to grow.

People who are connected as a result of being on a team are more faithful, more committed, and less likely to leave the church. If the only time the team spends together is working, they will not be very connected. Having individual team gatherings that are socially inspired rather than task-oriented helps people form friendships within the church.

8. *The best recruiters are not the leaders, but the other team members.* Teach team members to invite and welcome others to be a part of the team. Granger Community Church in Granger, Indiana, led by pastors Tony Morgan and Tim Stevens, teaches an approach called "shoulder tapping," which trains every member to think of it as their responsibility to tap the shoulders of folks they know and invite them into ministry. Every volunteer has contacts that the team leaders and pastors don't have. This shoulder-tapping approach within the context of relationships is more natural than an appeal from the platform or a phone call from the team leader. It also creates teams of people who know each other and choose to work together.

Rather than a person volunteering on a team where they don't know anyone, the volunteer at least knows the person who tapped his or her shoulder. There is already a sense of belonging for the volunteer.

9. *Value your volunteers.* One of the best books I've read on leading volunteers is a book entitled *To Lead Is to Serve* by Shar McBee. I recommend it for all levels of church leaders. In her book, Shar tells how a state agency wanted to hire a full-time volunteer coordinator. In order to justify the cost, the agency did a study to determine the value of volunteers. The results showed that, in general, the benefits of volunteers were at least six times greater than the cost. For every dollar spent on supervising volunteers, six dollars in services were received from them. In terms of time alone, one hour spent by a staff member in supervising volunteers produced nine hours of volunteer work.

In a similar study, the Tacoma Rescue Mission, Tacoma, Washington, discovered they receive the equivalent of 1.2 million dollars annually in volunteer work. Churches who implement a team church approach to involving members in ministry not only multiply resources, but they also help members fulfill their need to be involved in the church.

High-Five teams are the life of our volunteer ministry at Champions Centre. Every member is given the opportunity to release their God-given gifts and strengths to serve others for the purpose of building the church and impacting the community. We provide ministry preparation to help individuals determine the ministry that will best fit their gifts and talents. Discovering the spiritual gifts and personality types takes their confidence to a higher level.

Our High-Five teams come in all sizes and shapes, and more people participate in these volunteer teams than in any of our other small groups. Placement in a High-Five team begins in Joining the Team Class 101 and continues into Team Placement Class 201 where new members discover their gifts and select a team to be a part. The High-Five theme represents giving a minimum of five hours a month to your high calling. The theme Scripture is from Philippians 3:14 (paraphrased): "I press toward the mark of my high calling." Of course, some people volunteer much more than five hours a month, but there should be many more opportunities that can accommodate those who can only make a minimal time commitment as a volunteer.

10. *It is extremely important that team leaders see their main goal as helping everyone in the church find a place on a team.* Team leaders should work together for that purpose versus competing to get everyone on his or her own team. Volunteers will guard themselves from being taken advantage of when they sense that team leaders have only their own interests in mind. On the other hand, volunteers also sense when the team leader wants to help them find the right

place on a team, so they can have an enjoyable, fulfilling experience.

When the volunteer senses that a team leader just wants to help them use their God-given gifts, their defenses go down and their commitment goes up. Volunteers who do not enjoy what they do can at the very least feel appreciated for their willingness to serve. If they want to try serving on another team, they should be encouraged to do so without feeling condemned. Again, the main goal is to have *everyone* on a team.

➤ Strategies for Leading Successful Teams

To generate enthusiasm and commitment for our teamwork, we have a monthly Team Church Rally Night. This night is the hub of organization and ongoing inspiration for volunteers at our church. We hold it on one evening a month, beginning with department team meetings that are held all over our campus. During these one-hour organizational meetings, new team members are welcomed, given updates, informed, and trained for serving on the team.

The individual team meetings are followed by a one-hour fun rally at 6 p.m. with all the teams coming to the main auditorium for a celebration of awards, progress reports, and a brief (20-30 minutes) team-building message from me or another pastor. Those are the two most dynamic and important hours of the team-building effort at our church.

An effective way our team leaders equip our volunteers is through orientation and role-playing at these monthly meetings. Everyone who volunteers should first attend a team orientation before serving on the team. At the training meeting, they will receive:

- Clearly defined goals of the team
- Introduction to team leaders
- Schedules
- Reporting methods
- Expectations of the team leader and team members.

We have made it the goal of our volunteer ministry to develop a standard that no one is asked to do anything in ministry without rehearsing it first. Here are some reasons why role-playing helps build an effective team.

Role-playing forces the leader to think out exactly what volunteers are expected to do. The choir has a rehearsal, so why shouldn't ushers? Prayer partners? Information teams? Rehearsals require leaders to communicate what they want the team to do, and it also allows them practice doing it. How much more effective could teams be if leaders were communicating and rehearsing their roles with them?

Rehearsal gives a volunteer the security of knowing they know what to do. No one has to figure out the next step alone or fear not knowing exactly what to do. Through role-playing, volunteers gain the confidence they need to do their work effectively.

Role-playing in order to practice preserves the culture you have carefully designed. If we don't show volunteers how we want something done, we leave it open to be done "any old way." Any old way may not be consistent with the standard of excellence and cultural style of your design.

Don't be intimidated by role-playing at the orientation meetings. The idea is to simply give examples of possible scenarios that volunteers may encounter. Format your role-playing in a way that is easy for a trainee to understand and remember. Use acronyms, rhymes, or logical sequences such as the Smile Approach to teach greeters and ushers how to put visitors at ease:

Smile
Make a shake
Introduce yourself
Learn their name
Eye contact

After explaining the memory tag of the Smile Approach, show your team how it looks by greeting one of them. In other words, tell them, show them, watch them, and coach them.

It is best to write instructions, then show an example, watch the volunteers practice role-playing, and then coach them with any additional suggestions.

Above all, make training sessions and service times fun and encouraging for everyone who participates. Lead the group to cheer for each other and encourage one another during role-playing. And rehearse often. All team members must understand that what you train them to do are Standard

Operating Procedures. The monthly refresher course will keep everyone connected and focused on how to maintain the refreshing church culture you have designed for the purpose of presenting a positive, life-giving message to a lost and dying world.

Conclusion

> ## Teamwork Makes God's Dream Work

Now, imagine that it is early Sunday morning and prime time for team church. People come of all ages, economic status, race, and gender, but they all arrive as individuals ready to be part of a team. They have different roles, but they share a common goal. Teams huddle together for last-minute instructions and prayer, and then they are off to various posts of duty.

It's Game Day at church, and members are offering themselves and their talents to something bigger than they are. They will welcome people, provide classes for children, serve coffee, park cars, play instruments, operate lights and cameras, provide security, solve a host of unexpected problems . . . and much, much more.

Some of the team may have begun to serve at the Saturday night service, and others will arrive early Sunday morning to help set up for the big event of worshipping the Lord together. These team members are the real heroes of our local churches. They are ordinary people, who are doing extraordinary things. Together, they are making God's dream work . . . through teamwork. They are the ones who stood up, left the bleachers, and joined the team. They are God's Dream Team Church.

As you complete this book, I'm sure you realize by now that the seven practices, explained in each chapter, that create church culture are intended to work together to create a sum greater than its parts. I trust that you also realize that my goal has not been to tell you what your church culture should be in terms of *style,* as much as what it should be in terms of *spirit* and *substance.*

As church leaders, we have both the privilege and responsibility to put points on the board and run up the score in favor of the church in this generation. I not only hope for your ministry success, but I also hope you experience a fantastic and enjoyable run as you do your part to build God's church. Paul wrote:

> Live a lover's life, circumspect and exemplary, a life Jesus will be proud of: bountiful in fruits from the soul, making Jesus Christ attractive to all, getting *everyone* involved in the glory and praise of God (Philippians 1:10–11 MSG).

When the apostle Paul wrote his letters to the early church, he was fully aware of his mission on earth and completely committed to staying in the game until his mission was complete. With that same awareness of our mission and an eternal commitment to its cause, let's encourage as many people as possible to get off the bleachers and into the game!

Notes

Chapter 2

1. Robert Premeaux, "Duke's Coach K Understands How to Motivate," *The Bryan/College Station Eagle,* 26 April 2005, http://www.aggiesports.com/columnists/premeaux/042605premeaux.htm.
2. Walton, Sam, and John Huey. 1993. *Sam Walton, Made in America: My Story.* New York: Bantam Books.
3. Ibid.
4. "DisneySpeak." Wikipedia, The Free Encyclopedia. http://en.wikipedia.org/wiki/DisneySpeak (accessed August 24, 2006).
5. Wilson, J. Q. and G. E. Kelling. 1982. "Broken Windows: The Police and Neighborhood Safety." *Atlantic Monthly,* March. http://198.170.117.218/pdf/broken.pdf (accessed September 1, 2006).
6. "Rudolph Guiliani," Academy of Achievement. http://www.achievement.org/autodoc/page/ giu0bio-1 (accessed September 1, 2006).
7. Zagat Survey: New York City Marketplace Survey 1999.
8. Gerald, Kevin. *Developing Confidence* (Tulsa: Insight Publishing, 2003) 14.

Chapter 5

1. Pike Place Fish, "What Bizfutures Means to Us," http://www.pikeplacefish.com/philosophy/philosophy.htm (accessed July 14, 2006).

Chapter 6

1. Salary increases for the staff are best delegated to a remnant of the council and reviewed twice yearly. The pastor's salary is best determined with outside participation of other pastors and advisors.
2. The Institute for Motivational Living, "IML Company Profile," http://www.discinsights.com/ cyber/scripts/company.asp (accessed July 14, 2006).
3. Today in the Word, MBI, August, 1991, p. 16. www.bible.org.

Chapter 7

1. Cohn, Linda. 2000. Women in the Workforce: They Have Come a Long Way. http://www.businessweek.com/bwdaily/dnflash/feb2000/nf00215a.htm *Business Week Online* (accessed September 14, 2006).
2. Ibid.

Chapter 8

1. Malcolm Gladwell, *The Tipping Point: How Little Things Can Make a Big Difference* (New York: Back Bay Books, 2002).
2. Nations Volunteer Association. Tacoma Rescue Mission multiplied the volunteer hours that were logged at their site with the amount of money the NVA said those volunteer hours were worth.

About the Author

Kevin Gerald is best known for his communication of practical, biblical principles that empower people to live successful Christian lives. He is the founder and Senior Pastor of Champions Centre, one of the largest congregations in the Pacific Northwest. Thousands are exposed to his relevant teaching of the Bible through his local and international television program, *Building Champions for Life*. Kevin and his wife Sheila reside in Puyallup, Washington, and they have one daughter, Jodi.

Access to Kevin Gerald's books and teaching materials can be found at www.kevingerald.com.